BST

ALLEN COUNTY PUBLIC LIBRARY

3 1833 05507 7553

THE MAN'S

- ✓ Poker Secrets
- ✓ Beer Lore
- ✓ Waitress Hypnosis
- ✓ And Much, Much More!

Gregg Stebben

stained -5/24/12 (TAD

CIRCULATING WITH THE LISTED PROBLEM (S) :

With an Introduction by Denis Boyles

Skyhorse Publishing

Copyright © 2008 by Denis Boyles

All Rights Reserved. No part of this book may be reproduced in any manner without the express written consent of the publisher, except in the case of brief excerpts in critical reviews or articles. All inquiries should be addressed to Skyhorse Publishing, 555 Eighth Avenue, Suite 903, New York, NY 10018.

Skyhorse Publishing books may be purchased in bulk at special discounts for sales promotion, corporate gifts, fund raising, or educational purposes. Special editions can also be created to specifications. For details, contact Special Sales Department, Skyhorse Publishing, 555 Eighth Avenue, Suite 903, New York, NY 10018 or info@skyhorsepublishing.com.

www.skyhorsepublishing.com

10 9 8 7 6 5 4 3 2 1

Library of Congress Cataloging-in-Publication Data

Stebben, Gregg.
    The man's manual : poker secrets, beer lore, waitress hypnosis, and much, much more / Gregg Stebben.
        p. cm.
    Includes bibliographical references and index.
    ISBN-13: 978-1-60239-241-0 (alk. paper)
    ISBN-10: 1-60239-241-2 (alk. paper)
    1. Men—Psychology. 2. Men—Conduct of life. I. Title.

HQ1090.S87 2008
646.70081—dc22

                            2007048994

Printed in China

CONTENTS

FOREWORD

First, a word of congratulations. Buying this book was a stroke of genius. Maybe it was even your stroke of genius! Or maybe it was a gift from someone you know—and the chances are very good she was (and no doubt still is) a woman.

If so, she may be sending you a message—and of course, we'll listen, since, as men, we try to be whatever works, woman-wise. For example, it's been four decades since the advent of the "New Man." Odious at birth, he was a wimpy Ken to feminism's in-your-face Barbie, a quiet, well-mannered, non-threatening kind of chap with a shaved chest, marinated in estrogen and programmed to stay out of the way. Over the years, he morphed again and again. One day, he was Phil Donahue, the next Alan Alda. By the '90s, he was every Manhattanite's best man, the elfin Metrosexual. In one guise or another, the New Man's been around so long, he's old—and not in a good way.

Is there a good way to be an Old New Man? As it happens, yes. Because if recent news reports are correct, the women of the future are likely to closely resemble women of the distant past. Isn't it just a cruel accounting hoax that would allow the nineteenth century to follow the twentieth? Yet, according to a recent *New York Times* story filed by a correspondent at Yale, "Many women at the nation's most elite colleges say they have already decided that they will put aside their careers in favor of raising children [and] play a traditional female role, with motherhood their main commitment." As one particularly alarming Yale professor put it, "Women today are, in effect, turning realistic."

That's the problem with modernity. It gets old very quickly. And this latest thing—well, obviously, it's not great for some of us. For a long time now there has been a happy assumption among men that a brave new breed of highly educated, richly employable women were walking the Earth, women who wouldn't dream of putting "aside their careers in favor of raising children," when they could just hire somebody who had made a career of raising other people's children to do it for them.

From a somewhat cynical, perhaps even misogynistic point of view, marrying one of those beautiful breadwinners in order to better buy boats, beer and a Beemer made complete sense. Their incomes often exceeded those of the men who pursued them; a winning suitor would take not just the hand of his beloved, but also the purse clutched tightly in that hand. In return, her supportive husband would watch the game on Sunday, pay somebody to mow the yard on Saturday and encourage her to ask for raises. A woman at work meant a man at ease.

No more. Now women have decided to "play a traditional role" and are therefore "turning realistic."

That means new marching orders for us. And that's where the genius of buying this little book comes in. Many realistic women are going to prefer realistic men—i.e., a male who can actually function in the realistic world, where boats capsize, tires go flat, ties go wide and where a fellow's accomplishments are measured in his ability to help a woman lead the traditional, realistic life she wishes to lead. Goodbye to all that we used to be—lovable chunks of meat, talking sex objects, bronzed love gods. Hello to what we must now become—a handy man, a traditional guy who can do real stuff.

If you're seeking some reality, this book is the place to start. Hold it in your hand. Feel that heft? It's a real book—not a plastic screen or a txt msg on ur fone. The pages are made from butchered trees once filled with birds' nests and every word in it was typed *by hand*, then arranged neatly on each page in a way that conveys hundreds and hundreds of useful tips, hints and insights, all of practical value in the real world where those realistic women live. Need to know how to tie a bowline? It's here. Want to check the quality of a suit? Look on page 27. The pilot of your 747 just die in mid-air? Landing instructions are in

Chapter 5. This book can make you look exactly like a man who knows what he's doing.

Don't think you can just wait out this unpleasant little reversal in the universal hope of all men to live as cheap, unskilled chattel waiting on the pleasure of the attractive, intelligent women of the future who will keep us in the manner to which we avidly wish to become accustomed. It took forty years for the women at *Yale* to realize that we're happy to take them for granted if they so insist. But it's going to take them a lot longer than that to want that kind of guy back again. He's history.

But this book isn't. Unlike a wide tie or a huge SUV or a New Man, this book's for keeps. She's happy she got it for you. You can thank her by building a bookcase then painting the house.

Denis Boyles

1. Hardware and Machinery

The reason a man's life starts with hardware and machinery is that most men's lives are like complicated machines with plenty of moving parts. Most of the time, life just hums along. But one day, you hear a cough and a sputter, and suddenly there's smoke and fire everywhere. That's when it pays to know a little about hardware, because once you understand hardware, the only thing standing between you and bliss is finding the right tool for the job.

Hardware

HOW TO PUT TOGETHER ANYTHING

Here's the bad news on that analog 12G5 widget you just had to have: The elbows at the top of pole assemblies 12 and 14 go *inverse* to the cross-member and motor-mount housing. Who knew?

Well, maybe you knew. But most normal guys would assume that if you reverse those pole assemblies on the 12G5, and then wind her up, what you get is your basic torqued-widget fault, in which the widget pod, instead of going front to back, goes wonky in a kind of front-to-side-to-upside-down motion, real fast. Cool, huh?

Other more widget-savvy guys hate that stuff, though. They'll come along behind you with a pair of pliers and straighten out all the pieces you had carefully reengineered to fit the way you thought they were supposed to fit.

You may think the lesson in this little tale is that it always pays to read the directions, but you're wrong. The lesson here is that there are only so many ways to put together *anything,* and that once these fundamental principles of what we can call civilian engineering have been mastered, there is nothing you cannot join together, no assembly you cannot assemble, no tabs you cannot insert, no slots you cannot fill, no act you can't get together.

What follows are:

The Master Assembly Instructions

After you read these directions once—design flaws, emotional trauma, and manufacturing errors notwithstanding—*you'll never have to read any directions for anything ever again.*

GET THE BIG PICTURE

This is the most important step of all, which is why it comes first: ***Look at the box.***

No matter what you're putting together, the parts look nothing like the whole. If you spread out the parts for the 12G5, for instance, you'd think it was something you, personally, might like—a sit-down vaulting pole, for instance (would that be *great* or what?) where you could just, like, run along until you got to the thirty-foot crossbar, plant your pole, take a seat, and ride the crest in style, waving to the crowd and taking pictures as you go—instead of whatever it is for the tyke. One look at the box will set you straight.

This particular assembly instruction—looking at the box—is critical because it has universal application. To illustrate why, let's take something not normally associated with hardware. For instance, you take Mexico and a cheeseburger and put them together, you wouldn't think you'd get a taco. You have to see it before you can build it. Like a field of dreams.

Use Your Mental Wrench. So look at the picture, imagine how it's assembled, then, mentally, *disassemble* the thing. In fact, a good set of instructions contains an exploded diagram. That's really all you need. Spill all the parts out of the box onto a smooth surface—the floor, maybe. Place them on the living room carpet so they appear in the order shown on the exploded diagram. From here on, it's just a matter of tightening things up. (But not too tight.)

RECOGNIZE A LIE WHEN YOU SEE IT
Unless nature has blessed you with a Phillips-head fingernail, you *always* need tools, always, no matter what. Just in case, better get power tools. New ones, and lots of them.

DON'T READ THE DIRECTIONS
Except, of course, those you're reading just now. You already knew this one, right? Besides, the people who write directions do not make the objects the assembly of which they describe. They know much less about how to put something together than you will five minutes after you finish the job. Why? Because engineers can't write worth a damn, and because writers can barely assemble their thoughts, let alone something as complicated as a Soloflex.

An Exception: Always read the instructions accompanying any product made in China, for, while the directions apparently have nothing to do with the product, they do provide a great deal of admirable practical advice. An example, from a package of bottle rockets made in the People's Republic: "1. Point up to cloudy sky. 2. Match fire will ignite fuse. 3. Do not hover. 4. Listen carefully for report."

IF YOU'RE CONFUSED, SIZE THE PARTS

When you're putting something together, remember there are *three basic types of parts out of which all unassembled products are made:*

1. Little parts.
2. Really important parts, including the Main Thing.
3. Big parts.

The key to proper assembly is to start small and work your way up.

The Little Parts. You can't skip the small stuff. This causes frustration, I know, but here it is: Little pieces almost always have to be put together before big pieces. Except in *Mad Max* movies, most assembled objects do not have their innards hanging on the outside. As a rule, the little stuff gets put together in small assemblies. These, in turn, become part of a larger assembly.

It's the little things in a big thing that make everything go a little more smoothly. In that regard, little things do indeed mean a lot. Take sex, for instance. For most of us, it's a big thing, yes? But without that little thing, you got nothing.

The Really Important Parts. What we mean here is the one piece—technically, the Main Thing—without which no other piece will be able to stay in place. The L'il Tad 12G5 has that wicked crossmember, for example. That's the thing you have to worry about, because if you get that wrong, nothing else will be right.

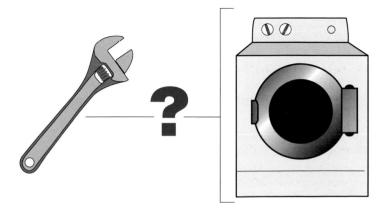

Every Assembly Has a Main Thing That Holds Together All the Other Things.

Witness:

- Washing machines: Tub armature. If the tub armature bends, no more whiter than white.
- Wagons: The axles. If an axle's upside down, those tires are goners.
- Balkan conflicts: Crazy Serbs. Crazy Croats. No Croats, no Serbs, no war.

There's always one thing that makes sense of everything else. Find it, feel it, understand it. It's the key to your universe.

Assembly tip: How to spot the Main Thing. It's usually a medium-sized piece, not the biggest, and not one of the little pieces of shrapnel stapled in the little plastic bag. There's usually a hole in it—often, two, one at each end.

Big Parts. Here's an important rule about big parts:

THE BIG THING ISN'T NECESSARILY THE MAIN THING

In fact, the biggest thing is often the least consequential, because it simply wraps up everything else. On a car, for instance, the hood is a big thing, but it certainly isn't any of the main things that make the car go. Since, in most assemblies, the Main Thing is usually the thing that takes up the most room, you'll want to get it out of the way first. Trying to put together the Big Thing first is an understandable mistake, of course, since by putting together the Big Thing first, you'll also make a giant step toward making all those parts look like that picture. But here's a promise: If you build the Big Thing first, you'll have to take it apart when you start building all the little things. Then you'll have to dismantle everything when you finally figure out the Main Thing.

A note on electronic stuff: Everything that has to do with electronic goods comes in pairs. It's a yin-yang thing. Every part is a positive or a negative, a red or a gray, an input or an output. Abstractly, these things all form a big circle that isn't complete until all the positives and negatives are joined together. To assemble any pile of electro-junk, all you have to do is keep track of the pluses and the minuses. You have to keep the inputs going in and the outputs going out.

TIGHTEN NOTHING UNTIL IT'S ALL OVER

Tightening all the screws and bolts is the last thing you do in any assembly process. Give everything a little elbow room, let it all settle. Once you're sure, then you can commit.

How to Hammer a Nail

If you're looking for the animal tracks of a previous generation, start here. At no other time in the history of man have so few men known so little about such a completely obvious thing as how to drive a nail into a board. If you know, fine. You're a manly man. If you don't, keep it to yourself—and learn this three-step process:

Step one: Drill it, dull it, drive it. If the nail is going to be driven anyplace where it's likely to split the wood, drill a small pilot hole first. If you're on the fence about the likelihood of splitting the wood, buy some insurance by turning the nail upside down and tapping it a few times on the point. A dull nail is far less likely to split wood than a sharp one.

Step two: Set the nail. Hold it between your thumb and forefinger and give it a sure-thing tap. Don't girl out on this: Hit the thing hard enough that you're not going to have to set it again. You want it to stand up all by itself.

Step three: Nail it. Hold the hammer at the end of the handle. Keep your wrist fairly stiff, and whack it. You use your whole forearm for this: A good hammer blow is very much like a good overhead slam in tennis. You want to pound right *through* the nail's head. Practice this for five minutes, and you should be able to set an eightpenny nail with one tap and drive it into a two-by-four with three good, solid, no-jive shots.

Notes: Lots can happen between the first tap and the last whack:

- If you bend the nail more than a little, don't fool with it. Yank it out and take it from the top.
- Don't miss. There are two telltales of a bum carpenter: bent nails, of course, and scarred wood. If you see a nail head surrounded by what appear to be miniature elephant tracks, you know a rube has been at work.

- If the wood's green, or if it's ungodly hard, soap the tip of the nail with a bar of Ivory.
- If you're doing any kind of finish work, don't drive the nail home with the hammer. Instead, hold it back from the surface of the board a bit and use a nail punch to finish the job.

How to Keep Your Thumbnail on Your Thumb After You Whack It with a Hammer

This really works:

Step one: Whack your thumb with a hammer while you're trying to drive in a nail.

Step two: Gas it. Before you can count slowly to thirty, get your thumb under a can of gasoline.

Step three: Slowly trickle gasoline over the banged-up thumbnail. You don't need a gush of gas; a trickle slow enough to last about a minute will do the trick. No blue nail, no aching thumb.

Step four: Stop smoking.

Once you figure out how to drive in a nail, take your knowledge to grad school.

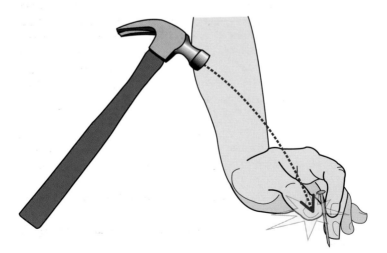

How to Perform Stupid and Life-Threatening Tricks with Nail Guns

Hey, here's some good news: You can do anything with a nail gun that you can do with a .22, including lots of truly terrifying and dangerous stunts. A correspondent has sent us some of his faves.

Before you can play any of these games you have to disassemble the safety on your gun. It's designed to ensure that you only nail into something solid, so it requires that you be pressing the nose of the gun down onto a rigid surface before you fire it. Every safety is different. Unload your gun and then give it the once-over: You'll figure something out. What you've got to do is figure out how to press down on the safety and hold it there as if the nose were pressed against a solid surface while you are swinging it around in the air looking for something to shoot.

NAIL GUN SPORTS

- ***Shoot the lackey.*** Every construction site has a lackey. Take turns shooting at him as he goes about his chores. Make sure he isn't close enough that it would hurt if you actually hit him, and make sure you don't aim for the eyes. Deduct points if you shoot at him while he has run off to get you a beer.

- ***Target shooting.*** Put up a wedding photo from your first marriage or a snapshot of the site foreman. Fire away. Bull's-eye wins. With a nail gun you've got, say, thirty feet. Therefore, when you aim you have to aim high because the nail will go straight for only a foot or two and then start dropping. In a way, that means you can have a lot more fun with a nail gun because you can fire it off over here and not worry about hitting some lady sitting in her living room a half mile away.

- ***Indoor skeet shooting.*** One guy throws up a chunk of wood, the other guy draws and shoots. If you're a little slow on the upswing, play with a Styrofoam coffee cup; it will float to the ground much slower and therefore be much easier to draw a bead on.

- ***Pest control.*** Mouse or rat or—if you're working construction in the Bronx—cockroach hunting.

- ***Catch.*** You hold the gun, your buddy tries to catch the nails in his base-ball glove.

A small note: While we're pleased to get tips and hints on how to make the workday go a little faster, we really don't recommend any of these fascinating pastimes. In fact, hard to believe, but the lackey-shoot might even be illegal. It's an OSHA thing.

HOW TO HIDE THE HANDWRITING ON THE WALL

Don't confuse painting a wall with painting a masterpiece. The difference between a wall painted by a household Picasso and the one you paint yourself is minimal. Just get it covered.

Latex, Please

Unless you have a specific need for enamel paint, skip it. The prep work and the cleanup are mindless time-eaters. Latex paint is the best thing to happen to paintbrushes since Tom Sawyer cut his toe.

How much latex paint should you buy? The rule of thumb is one gallon of paint per 450 square feet of wall space. That's assuming you can do the job in a single, thick coat.

For next to nothing, you can buy one of those cheap, plastic kid's pools downtown. For a big painting job, just fill the wading pool with water and toss the brushes, trays, and rollers into the pool as you go. Give everything a final squirt with the hose when you're ready to go.

By the way, if you end up using enamel despite our warnings and you get some of the paint on your skin, olive oil will take it right off. Works with latex, too, of course.

How to Prepare a Wall

- *Scrape off loose paint* with a scraper or putty knife.
- *Use spackle* to fill in holes and cracks, and to smooth out dents and rough spots. Even old paint can make a wall too rough to paint.
- *Sand down all rough surfaces.* A coat of primer on sanded spots will save you two coats of paint later.
- *Cover water-stained areas with a stain killer.* Stains on walls live forever, and unless you "seal" them, they'll show through the new coat of paint as well as they do through the old paint.
- *Remove all dust* from the walls, ceiling, and floors. Painting over dust is begging for trouble.
- *Cover window and door sashes with masking tape.* If you're painting down close to a narrow baseboard, remove the trim. Then tape newspaper along the floor and an inch or two up the wall so that when you replace the baseboard, only new paint will show.

How to Paint a Wall

- *Take it from the top*—ceiling first. Use a brush to paint a narrow strip around the perimeter of the ceiling.
- *Load the roller* with paint evenly, but be sure it is not saturated to the point where it will drip. If you see a thick bead of paint along the edge of the roller's track of color, you're using too much.
- *Work in small patches.* Cover three or four square feet at a time in a zigzag motion—first away from you and then back to cover the parts you missed. Once you have covered several adjoining patches, crisscross over the entire area to make sure that the paint is applied uniformly over each section.
- *Always paint toward the light source,* never painting more area than you can easily reach. Faraway chunks of wall tend to get short shrift, so move your ladder frequently. Start in a dry area and work toward an area that has already been painted. If you try to do it the other way around and feather the color out toward the unpainted part of the wall, you'll only create a big patch of paint surrounded by lots of barely painted wallboard.
- *Use a brush* not only to paint around the edges of the wall at the ceiling, but also in the corners and around doors and windows.

- *Shield it.* If the color you are painting is different from that on the other walls or the ceiling, use a piece of cardboard to protect those surfaces as well as moldings and baseboards.
- *To avoid drips,* make sure the first stroke after you reload the roller is an upward one.
- *Work quickly*—or as quickly as you can without making a huge mess. Semidry paint looks different from wet paint, so if you work at a brisk pace, you'll have a much easier time judging how much paint you need to cover the wall and where touch-ups are needed.

If wall painting is too *basic,* too mundane, too down-to-earth, you can elevate your newfound hardware expertise with this small exercise in aeronautical engineering.

HOW TO BUILD A BOMBER USING A MATCHSTICK AND A BUNCH OF FROZEN FLIES

This is the kind of handyman derring-do that made America great:

- *Take a wooden matchstick* and slice a thin sliver down one side. Then cut the remaining stick in two, lengthwise. Make sure you leave a little of the red tip intact for effect. Discard half the 'stick.
- *Make the aircraft* by gluing the sliver of wood—the wing—across the remaining part of the matchstick—the fuselage. If you want, you can use little scraps to make a tail section. Or you can make a biplane. Or you can use a couple of thin slices of balsa to make a huge wing, one that will carry maybe *twenty* engines. Indulge your aeronautical whims. Think of lift, think of thrust, think of innovation without the benefit of an industrial policy.
- *Catch a bunch of flies.* Put them in a jar and put the jar in the freezer. In a few seconds, the flies will be chilled out completely. (Male honeybees also work swell, but sexing bees can be tricky work.) This is called cryogenics, and it has its drawbacks. For example, the flies will be *dead flies* if you freeze them for too long. Dead flies are no good. So if you're a slow tinkerer, simply refrigerate your flies. It takes longer to make them comatose, but they have a much higher rate of recovery than the ones you leave in the freezer.

- *Meanwhile, put a tiny drop* of rubber cement at each place along the wing where you want an engine.
- *Take the flies out of the freezer.* Attach the abdomen of one frigid fly to each drop of glue. Make sure all the flies are facing the same direction.
- *Breathe life into the flies.* A miracle: A gentle puff of your warm breath will resuscitate the flies.
- *Launch the aircraft.* It should fly like a charm, and, far from being cruel to the flies, you'll be teaching them a new and valuable thing, one which brings us to the virtue of this exercise. For we see that while flies have a great deal in common, think a lot alike, share many hopes and dreams, they never act in concert, as a team, with regard for the worth of other, neighboring flies, *until forced by grim circumstance*—as, for example, when they are harnessed to fly and either first experience the exhilaration of high-altitude cooperation or die. Redeemed by such a critical choice, they'll soar like a glider, race like a Stealth, and, when overflying a barnyard or kennel, turn into an awesome-wicked dive-bomber.

Machinery

When you combine hardware with a full tank of gasoline, you get an alchemy all men understand. For when it comes to essential information, there are some things guys just *know*. For example, men *know* baseball, the same way they *know* how to change tires in the rain while maintaining a casual conversation with their wives, the way they can make a clothesline peg from third to first without warming up, the way they can kill anything that flies or crawls, the way they can operate anything that burns gas or oil. Right? Somewhere in our genetic baggage, there's an old manual that contains the instructions to all these things, and if we've lost track of it, well, who needs directions, anyway? Right?

Right—up to a point. In fact, it's the common acceptance of what must be called manly skills that sharpens the competitive edge among men and makes them hotdog like maniacs in front of women.

Take heavy equipment.

You get two guys standing around a tractor, and you get big-time testosterone-talk. Chain saws do this, too. So do motorcycles, welding tools, and pit bulls. Backhoes do it big-time. Men were *born* to backhoe. Blenders and juicers would do it if they were powered by Briggs & Stratton eight-horse-power OHV single-stroke engines and had a decent transmission. In fact, anything in the physical world not feminized is contested territory among men—especially if there are women around.

HOW TO MAKE THE EARTH MOVE

Now, a tractor is a loud, massive piece of machinery dedicated to the constructive exercise of *power*. Men understand work, and tractors are built for work, *ergo* real men understand tractors. Big Olivers and old Hart-Parrs, modern Deeres and lightweight Kubotas are beautiful pieces of iron and steel. Guys slap the metal on these monsters the way they grip a brother's shoulder. They're big, strong, and *functional*. Like Brigitte Nielsen, I guess. Around heavy equipment, gauntlets are everywhere. One guy tosses the keys to the other guy and says, "Try her out?"

You're the other guy. What do you do?

Mount Up

The thing that gets guys who don't know heavy equipment in trouble is their expectation of speed. You'd think that because something's big and loud, it ought to have speed, too. But that's where you'd go wrong. Any man can drive any piece of equipment if he just takes his time. It's all in what kind of expectations you have. When it comes to heavy equipment, just don't expect speed.

Skid shovels, 'dozers, and other kinds of grading equipment—stuff that pushes: Work slowly, from top to bottom. Say you've got a wall of dirt in front of you. You're not going to get far trying to dig from the bottom; you'll never lift the whole thing. So take it off the top, a bit at a time, and pretty soon you'll make a molehill out of that mountain.

A skid shovel lifts, a 'dozer pushes. But they both steer like a tank—with sticks that are essentially brakes used to stop the treads on one side of the machine or the other.

Backhoes and other similar kinds of excavation machinery can dig and lift. You're moving the arm up and down, scooping with the bucket, and turning the arm to drop what you've scooped. Go slowly, no matter how good you get. Some guys are like sculptors with these things. But they never hurry: Swinging a bucket into another guy's head will kill him *right now.*

The value of a backhoe can be determined by looking at two things: the hydraulics and the supports. Other stuff comes second. Tires, for example, don't matter at all.

Sod Busters

Farm tractors are the cabriolets of heavy equipment—kind of sporty compared to big, yellow earthmovers. Some general tractorial principles:

- *Gravity:* If you're pulling weight and you have to go downhill, use a gear one step lower than the one you think you'll need. If the weight starts pushing the tractor, whatever you do, don't step on the clutch. You'll only go flying. Most tractor accidents are caused by pulling too heavy a load behind too light a tractor. You're fine on level ground, but when you head downhill, you'll lose it.

- *Steer with the brakes*—one for the right wheel, one for the left—as well as with the steering wheel. In fact, you can drive a tractor with complete control using nothing but the brakes, provided you take it slow.

- *Narrow front-end tractors*—with a wheel configuration like a tricycle—are great for farming crops in rows. But you can flip one of these on level ground at five miles per hour by just turning too sharply.

The most perilous tractor is the Oliver 70, made from 1935 until the 1950s. The entire tractor—with the exception of the transmission pan—sits above the center of gravity.

Be especially cautious using a front-end loader on a trike tractor; lifting the bucket raises the center of gravity, and if you're on even a slight slope, you can flip. Wide front-end tractors are essential for utility work and for use on hilly ground.

HOW TO READ LIGHTS ON YOUR CAR'S DASHBOARD

They blink, you blink, and it's not love. It's trouble. But the trouble with idiot lights on a dashboard is they don't tell you what little they know. Not only are they idiot lights, they're flat outright *dumb.* If they could talk, though, here's what they'd say.

Hot

The message here is that the engine is, well, *hot.* Way too hot to drive, so pull over, shut it down, turn on the radio, and wait for exactly two innings.

Problem: The car's overheated because the engine isn't getting sufficient coolant. That's probably it. But it could also be overloaded; slow down, turn off the a/c, and see if that helps. No? Then it could be the thermostat.

What you do: When the motor cools down, open the radiator cap. If you do this before the engine's cool, you'll steam-blast the skin right off your face and spend the rest of your life looking like the front-page star of *Weekly World News.* So the first thing to check is the temperature of the engine. Is it cool? Cool. Check the water level; if you can see metal inside the radiator instead of fluid, you're dry. Need some water? Add some—but not until you've first checked all the hoses and belts. Grab the fan and try to wiggle it front-to-back. If it seems slightly loose, you need a new water pump. Medium bucks. Maybe it's the thermostat. You'll find it right where the big hose from the radiator comes into the engine. Check it out. If everything looks jake, but the car still overheats, don't drive it. Call Mr. Holmes. Never drive a car without coolant in it. You may get a mile or so down the road, but the whole engine will seize up and you'll be out of pocket a grand or two.

Alt

This means the alternator's not charging the battery. You can putt along for a few miles, but you're running on Delco alone, so don't press it.

Problem: Belt's loose. That's if you're lucky. If you're not, the belt's broken. Or the alternator's shot. If it's neither, the problem's in the electrical system. If you smell something weird in the engine compartment—say, burned wire insulation—take the keys out of the car so you don't accidentally put juice through the system, causing the damaged wire to spark, igniting the gas in the engine, spreading fire and mayhem through the car until the gas tank gets a flicker, then—you get the picture.

What you do: Replace the belt; replace the alternator; replace the wire. If the problem is just a loose belt, you can tighten it by using a wrench and a prying bar and a little common sense.

Oil

There's no oil. Don't drive.

Problem: Probably you. When was the last time you checked the oil?

What you do: Add some. Check the dipstick. If the level's still low, look under the car for the quart of oil you just poured in. Engines need oil to run. Don't try anything funny.

Brake

The emergency or parking brake is on.

Problem: The brake isn't releasing completely. Or maybe you're low on brake fluid.

What you do: Jiggle the brake handle. If that doesn't work, drive forward and backward a bit. Or, if you can spot it, check the emergency brake cable; on older cars—especially on older Ford trucks—the thing freezes up for no good reason. If none of this has any effect, check the brake fluid in the reservoir under the hood.

HOW TO DO DOWN-AND-DIRTY DIAGNOSTICS

If coolant flush were tea leaves, you'd know exactly what the immediate future holds for your jalopy. Here's how to read the alarming puddles of liquid tinder your broken-down car.

PUDDLE COLOR	LOCATION	DIAGNOSIS
Greenish bluish	Front end	Antifreeze. Something's leaking someplace—or you've overheated to the point where coolant is running out the vent. Keep the pooch away, incidentally. Dogs love lapping antifreeze. In fact, they *die* for it.
Black, dark brown	Front, probably	Oil leak. Check the plug on the oil pan.
Red	Front	Transmission or power-steering fluid. If it's tranny fluid, you'll probably see it leaking out from around the transmission fluid pan, just behind the car's oil pan. If it's power-steering fluid, you'll see it leaking out from one of the hoses running between the power-steering pump and the steering gearbox.
Clear	Anywhere	Hmm. Brake fluid's clear. Check the level in the master cylinder. Is it gasoline? Smell it. Gas leaks are a real mess—and dangerous, too. If you don't know how to track the fuel line and check the fittings, get it towed to somebody who does. Maybe it's just water. This is America's most common under-car puddle. Take the kids, load them in the car, drive around, and see for yourself: On a hot day, cars are dripping sweat like an indicted Arkansas banker. It's condensation from the air conditioner.
Clear	Anywhere	Could be windshield-washer solution. Check the reservoir. It's always made of plastic, so leaks aren't uncommon. Stuff's toxic, by the by.
Brown	Front	Power-steering juice, probably. Could also be oil. Could even be dirty water.
Yellow	Tires	Dogs.

TRANSPORTATION TOOL KIT

When you're on the road, your trunk should contain:
- A jack and a spare, of course.
- Jumper cables.
- A few wrenches, screwdrivers, and a pair of pliers.
- A quart of oil and a jug of windshield-cleaning solvent.
- Paper towels.
- Flashlight.
- Fire extinguisher.

  Semidissent: You're better off with an extinguisher *inside* the car.

HOW TO HAVE FUN WITH CHAIN SAWS

Hardware in bins may be fun. But you stick enough hardware together to make yourself a loud and dangerous machine, and, buddy, you're having man-sized fun.

This isn't a universal appreciation, by the way. In urban areas, danger isn't normally associated with machines. It's associated with lawyers and women. In fact, if you actually need evidence that it is no longer a man's world, allow me to point out that you could evacuate the entire New York Stock Exchange, turn the building upside down, and not find a single chain saw—proof the World of Work has been thoroughly feminized.

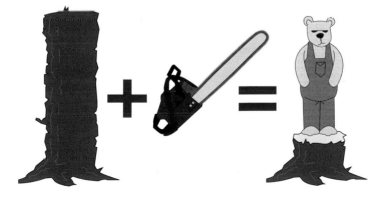

Outside Manhattan, where work actually involves *labor,* it's different. Chain saws are everywhere. Every guy's got a 'saw. I hang mine from my rearview. Guy down the road uses his as a key ring. We have lots of them because, even if we don't need them, we love them. Why? Well, for one thing, they're noisy. For another, they're dirty. And for another, they're *really* dangerous. And, for those city dwellers who may at this point be confused and in need of help to distinguish chain saws from bad wives, cranky bosses, and congressional Democrats, there's one other thing about chain saws: They're a good time.

How to Mop a Floor

Broom it out first. Don't fool around. Get a thirty-second aerobic workout. Stretch those arms, stretch those arms, move those legs, move those legs, then bend at the waist, one, two, hold it, breathe, start at the top, broom out the cobwebs in the corners. Knock all the dirt down to the floor.

TWO WAYS TO MOP

One way is to keep the water in the bucket and use the mop as a sort of big, wet dusting cloth. Cover the floor in three- to four-foot-square sections, keeping the exit from the room and the nearest sink to your back. When the mop gets dirty, rinse. When you reach the door, step out of the room and finish the job, then rinse your mop and leave it standing to dry with the mop-head up.

The other way is to grab a bucket of warm water and spill it here and there in the center of the floor. Work from the center out to three of the walls, keeping your line of retreat open. Soak it up, rinse it out, soak it up some more.

If you need a serious cleaning, use two mops and two buckets. First cover a section of the floor with water and a cleaning solution, then rinse that section with the second mop and plain water. Repeat.

A plug: Mop & Glo is a great one-step, bachelor-tested floor cleaner. It has been used under quasi-clinical conditions on industrial carpeting to remove beer scum, and it worked just fine.

How to Clean a Filthy Refrigerator

Let's say you, like our correspondent, won a refrigerator at a poker game. But then your father-in-law pointed out that if you took an appliance as filthy as that into your house, your wife—his daughter—would leave you and return to him. Here's what you do:

- *Load the refrigerator above the wheels* in the back of the pickup. Make sure it's secure, but you're going to need lots of room on all sides, so put it square in the middle of the bed. Don't lay a 'fridge on its side, either. Bad for the pipes.
- *Drive the 'fridge* to a do-it-yourself car wash.
- *Soap and steam* the refrigerator. Take your time, but five minutes ought to do the trick. Secure the door in an open position for the final leg of the trip home. Should be clean and dry by the time you hit the driveway. Feeling ambitious? Pop in a few more quarters and go to the next instruction.

How to Make a Bed So Tight You Can Flip a Quarter Off of It

- **Spread your bottom sheet** on the bed, and tuck all four corners in with a *hospital corner*. (Think of it as gift wrapping the mattress with the sheet.) Here are the four steps involved:

1. *Pull the sheet* real tight at the bottom of the bed, then push it under the mattress as far as you can. Tight, tight, *tight*.

2. *Go to the side,* where the sheet is hanging down. Pull the sheet out so it continues along the plane of the bed. Hold

it with one hand and take your other hand and push the fabric underneath the mattress.

3. *Make the first corner.* You should get some creases at the bottom of the bed and along the side.

4. *Repeat this process* on the other three corners of the bed, then tuck in whatever else of the sheet is left on the sides. Always tuck the sheet *as far under the mattress as you can.*

- ***Do the same with your top sheet,*** but only at the bottom of the bed.

- ***Spread your blanket*** over the top sheet. The top of the blanket should be a few inches from the top of the bed. Tuck the blanket in the same way you did the sheet at the bottom and along the sides.

- ***Pull the top of the top sheet*** down over the top of the top of the blanket. Tuck this part of the top sheet, which is doubled back on itself and the top of the blanket, under the mattress as well.

- ***Now, here's the trick:*** The way you make the sheets and blankets tight enough to bounce a quarter off is by *pinning the sheets and blankets under the bed to the mattress.* That's why it is always better to take the top bunk in the barracks. You can crawl all over the bed of the guy below you while you do this, but if you have the bottom bunk you've got to crawl under there and get all dirty. Anyway, you pull the sheets and blanket as tight as you can under the mattress from below the bunk, and then you safety-pin them to the mattress when they are pulled as tight as you can get them. Don't be stingy with the pins either; you'll need a lot of them to get all the way around the bed and keep everything pulled real tight.

How to Wash Your Car

This ought to be instinctive by now, yes? No. Our instincts are to do jobs such as this one as quickly and easily as possible. There's a better, if partially nonintuitive, way:

- ***Hose it.*** Wash the car down with plain water first to remove dust and loose dirt.

- *Soap it.* Choose a detergent with a low pH and cover the car thoroughly, starting, of course, at the top. If it's a hot day, and there's a chance the soap will dry on the surface, work in smaller areas.
- *Use only clean, soft cloths.* Even the smallest amount of dirt or grit can scratch the paint, especially on late-model cars.
- *Scrub tough spots* with baking soda or a soft plastic netlike dish scrubber.
- *Never wash your car in direct sunlight* or it will streak.
- *Rinse the car starting at the top* and working down.
- *Use commercial products to remove tree sap,* heavy bird droppings, gasoline and oil, and road tar.
- *Dry it.* Wipe your car clean with terry cloth towels.
- *Clean your windows* with undiluted vinegar. Rinse with water and dry with clean rags.
- *Clean the windshield wipers* with a cloth and a solution of water and antifreeze, mixed half-and-half.
- *Scrub the tires.* A touch of tire black helps. Clean, black tires make a huge difference to the appearance of a car.

2. Clothes

What crazy thing makes us get up every morning and put on a suit and tie? Perhaps the thought that if we didn't, we might think we were unemployed.

Suits, for instance, are admittedly a retro idea, the kind of cloak of anonymity many of us have been avoiding since the summer of 1967. But in an age of barbarous informality, where dressing "down" is seen as a progressive notion, suits can be a reassuring thing. Why? Because guys without jobs *never* wear suits.

So. Suits signify. A suit is the dress uniform of the working man. A suit says we are all dogfaces in the war on irresponsibility. We earn money. And we wear suits to prove it.

However, if we're all going to suit up, maybe we ought to take a sec to make sure we've got the right stuff—in the right size and in the right order—and that it's on the right way around.

How to Buy a Suit

You have three **Main Things:**
   1. Name.
   2. Price.
   3. Appearance.

Common sense screams, "Three!" while fear whispers, "Uno, bello, uno." So we split it down the middle and end up with neither.

WHAT'S IN A NAME?

A name on a suit is important to guys who wear "fashion"—as the tonier men's mags call what any regular guy would call expensive clothes. For most of us, there are only two reasons to buy a suit because of the name that's on it:
   1. *The contract says you have to.* If you make a deal to pitch for the Indians, the name on the suit's everything. But you'll notice Giorgio Armani doesn't have a franchise.
   2. *Proof of good taste.* The other reason to buy a suit because of the name on it is that you're an insecure guy who needs to be able to point to the "Giorgio" on the jacket lining so others will know that no matter what their eyes are telling them, you're actually well-dressed.

Either way, you get no guarantee the thing will fit. Here's the bottom line on **why the name on a suit means nothing:**

- *You can buy the name.* Lots of designers license their names to manufacturers and thereby sign away any control they have over what the suit looks like or how it fits.

- *The names you can't license,* ironically, are names such as Wal-Mart and other mass retailers. As many as three-quarters of all suits sold in the United States are sold in discount houses. Small wonder; the $99 suit you get down at SootCity may have started out as a $400 beauty at Nordstrom or Bloomie's. It may have survived a $200 tag at a specialty discount retailer, such as Men's Wearhouse, and ended up at the local discount barn for no worse reason than that the manufacturer made too many suits. On the other hand, the $99 suit you've been looking at may have started as a $1.25 suit in some remote corner of the Philippines or Ecuador.

HOW TO SPOT A CHEAP SUIT

Postcard from an honest haberdasher: "The same factory that makes a $600 suit also makes a $200 suit. And it's the same suit." Here's **how to tell if it's a good suit selling cheap** or a cheap suit worth exactly what you'll pay for it:

Wrinkles: There are two places where wrinkles matter. One is in the fabric itself; if you grab a handful of the material and crunch it, does it stay wrinkled? If it does, it's a cheap suit. Twisting an arm is a good way to gauge this, by the way.

Wrinkling of the fabric around seams is another surefire indicator of a ten-dollar prison-issue suit. Usually, it's a sign of cheap fabric *and* cheap manufacture, in which a robot machine made a seam by squirting a line of glue and squishing together all the layers of fabric. A guy in a glued-suit looks like Lurch. The only other way to finish a suit lapel is by hand. How to tell the difference? Rub the lapel between your thumb and forefinger. If the fabrics have a little play and rub against each other a bit, you're holding a hand-finished suit. If the lapel has no play, you're holding a fused-fabric special.

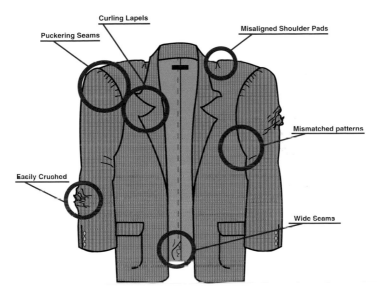

Curling Lapels

Misaligned Shoulder Pads

Puckering Seams

Mismatched patterns

Easily Crushed

Wide Seams

Count the stitches: A well-made garment will have a fairly dense stitch. If you can count more than twelve stitches to an inch of seam, you're okay. Less is bad; more is good.

Weave: Check the fabric under good light. See if there's a bunch of missing threads.

Match: Here's something else everybody forgets to check: Does the coat match the trousers? Very often, there are subtle differences because the two garments may be made by different third-world manufacturers—sometimes even on different continents.

Collar: Does the lapel lay flat, like it should, or does it roll and buckle, like it shouldn't?

The shoulder should lay neatly. The line of the shoulder seam should be flat, without waves or bulges.

The patterns should meet neatly at the shoulders, on the back, and under the arms. The pattern on the lapel and on the sleeve should match the pattern on the torso.

Lining: Except for all-cotton leisure wear, all suit jackets should be fully lined in the sleeves and at least halfway down the back. Trousers should be lined at least to the knee.

Fasteners: Check out the button that will hold your trousers closed. It should have a hand-finished loop behind it to keep it from popping off.

The buttons on a cheap suit will be—well, cheap looking. They'll also be loosely attached.

The sleeves on a cheap suit won't have a miter-cut to them. They'll be more like a shirt sleeve—and a lot harder to alter than a good suit sleeve.

The pockets on a good suit will have a coin pouch, and maybe other inside pockets.

Front: Look for a good French-fly front, with the drape of the cloth disguising any closures. It's a no-fail sign of a well-made suit of clothes.

HOW TO MEET YOUR MATERIAL NEEDS

Why Ray Charles Always Looks Cool

You can actually tell the difference between cheap fabric and expensive stuff by feel alone:

Cheap fabric is stiff and has a slight papery feel to it. When you put on a jacket made of cheap stuff, it hangs stiffly; sometimes, there's an unseemly crease at the bottom of the lapel; sometimes, the thing just hangs on you, like a drunk date.

The better the fabric, the softer it feels. Expensive suiting has a sort of springiness—a nonmale way of saying resilient flexibility. But don't get carried away with "springiness": A cheap fabric with a loose weave will possess more "springiness" than a cheap mattress.

The best fabric for a suit is worsted wool, which is to suiting material what aspirin is to drugs: a miracle. You can wear it in winter and stay warm, and in warm weather, the stuff breathes enough to keep you cool. Worsted wool also drapes better than most other fabrics.

Runners-up: If you weary of the usual worsted suit, try some of these alternatives:

- *For summer:* The standard beige or khaki summer suit (also called a "traveling suit") is a kind of classic and makes for a nice break in the worsteds. Avoid seersucker. A seersucker suit is what guys in the know call a "novelty suit."

A dissent: Cotton seersucker is a great fabric for summer suits. But be careful here: Seersucker is acceptable between Memorial Day and Labor Day, especially in hot-summer cities. But seersucker is to suiting material what bow ties are to neckwear: It's just a tad too cute for most men's lives. (More on bow ties later in this chapter.) If you have to get in touch with the frat-brat inside you by wearing suits with stripes of light blue, gray, or *pink,* then by all means make the suit a single-breasted number, make the shirt a solid Oxford-cloth button-down, and make the tie a Madras one. Add penny loafers, no socks. If you're going to go fey, go fey all the way.

- *For spring:* Silk and silk blends. Linen is also a good spring suit fabric. (But watch those wrinkles! See below.)
- *For winter:* Pure wool tweed is timeless—and wearless. A good tweed will last two lifetimes.

Linen Lament

Whoever said linen was a good hot-weather fabric must have been selling the stuff. The shapes of linen's peculiar fibers actually traps hot air. Silk does the same. Both of them wrinkle faster than a thumb in dishwater.

Synthetic Sympathy

Polyester blends help keep a suit looking fresh. Polyester also resists wrinkling. If you're a traveling kind of Wilbury, you can't do without a good poly-blend suit.

A dissent: If God had wanted us to wear chemicals, we'd all be wearing trash bags and runway foam. Polyester doesn't exist in nature. Adding it to a natural fabric, such as wool, is a great way to cheapen the appearance of a suit. If you're traveling and wrinkles are a worry, bring along one of those little fabric steamers, or take along a lightweight wool suit and let it hang in the john while you shower. Pure poly suits stick to your body. They stretch and bag, and look as cheap as they feel.

The Suit-to-Alteration Rule

Unless you're a peg-legged, piratical kind of guy, your new suit shouldn't need radical alterations. Assuming you've purchased something roughly your size, the most the store's tailor should have to do is hem the pants cuffs, adjust the waistband, fix the length of the sleeves, and, possibly, take in the jacket a bit under the arms or on the sides. That's it. So *if the store wants to charge you more than, say, fifty dollars for all this, you can take your business elsewhere,* safe in the knowledge that if it was willing to rip you off on the alterations, it was willing to rip you off on the suit, too.

CUFFS AND BUTTONS

Cuffs

Cuffs should never be thinner than an inch or wider than one and three-quarter inches.

Shorter men need shorter cuffs: If you're five-foot-ten or less, go for a cuff about an inch and a half wide.

Button Bits

The top button of a *two-button suit jacket* should button at the waist. No postmodern man wears a jacket with fewer than two buttons, of course, unless he's got his own lounge act. And no matter how many buttons *more* than two a jacket has, the bottom one is never buttoned.

Trad note: Button either the top two or just the middle button of a three-button suit coat.

How to Dress to Suit

A few notes from everywhere about how to wear a suit to achieve a specific effect:

- *Elegance:* If you want that 1940s sense of style and elegance, wear the waistband of your trousers just *slightly* above your actual waist—quite high on most men—and allow for a generous break in the trousers at the cuff. Wear your jacket buttoned, your tie tight. Your legs will look five yards long.

- ***Rough affability:*** Wear the waistband of your trousers well below your waist, so that if you actually had a beer gut, it would hang over your belt. Leave your jacket open and your tie loosely knotted.

- ***Serious competence:*** Most serious men are brain-dead, so dress like a mortician. Or like Dan Rather. Dark suits only. Wear the waistband of your trousers just ever so *slightly* below your waist. Hold it there with braces. Add a waistcoat when it's in style. But no matter what, keep your jacket buttoned. White shirts only, please, and make a small floral gesture with your necktie your only sign of life—plant or otherwise.

How to Take Care of a Suit

- ***Hanging hint:*** Always hang your suit jacket on a wooden or plastic hanger—the kind that offers a wide shoulder support and a slight curve forward at the shoulders. Your jacket will keep its shape twice as long.

- ***Hanging on empty:*** Don't leave stuff in your pockets when you hang up your suit coat. It'll just bag out *right now.* Also: Leave it unbuttoned when you hang it up. This allows the lapel to roll naturally.

- ***Don't crowd*** your suits in the closet. Give them some air and some space.

- ***Rotate:*** A suit should have forty-eight hours off for every twelve hours of work. It's like a union-suit thing. Letting the suit hang for a couple of days will restore the fabric, prevent bagging, and keep the suit looking fresh.

- ***Death press:*** When you take a suit or sport coat to the dry cleaners, always spend the extra two or three dollars to have it hand finished rather than run through the pressing machine. The pressing machine kills 50 percent of the garment. The heat causes the glue in a fused garment to separate, and it comes back puckered.

How to Dress for the Road

- **Pack right:** When packing, you can reduce the amount of clothing you have to take by sticking with the same three colors. If everything you take with you is blue, gray, and white, for instance, you can wear every shirt with every suit with every tie, and you'll have much more flexibility with your travel wardrobe.
- **Pack light:** If your business trip is for more than three days, take one less shirt and one less tie than you think you'll need.
- **Pack tight:** If you jam-pack your suitcase full of clothes, you'll end up with a wrinkled wardrobe at the other end of the plane ride. Better bet: Pack your suitcase tightly, but not jammed. If you leave too much room in your suitcase, you'll have the same wrinkled mess you'd have with a crammed 'case. A closely packed suitcase will keep clothes from bunching and wadding.

How to Dress for a Midnight—or Midlife—Crisis

Who came up with the idea that formal wear should be rented, but bowling shirts should be owned outright? *If you need a tux, buy the thing.* Why? Because there are at least **five more reasons to own one than the reason you think.**

You need your own tux:

1. to properly drink a martini;
2. to have something reasonable to wear on the beach at night;
3. to wear when driving a small, yellow convertible through Manhattan;

4. to add a small whiplash to a regular date with your wife;
5. to wear to breakfast the next morning.

HOW TO IDENTIFY THE PARTS OF A TUXEDO

This small list may seem obvious to some, but anyone who's ever seen a chap wearing a rented tux with a brand-new brown leather belt knows there's somebody out there who needs it.

- *Jacket:* The color should be black. Of the three collar styles available in most shops—peaked, pointed, or shawl—only the latter two are completely acceptable.

  Single-breasted jackets with a peaked lapel are the most versatile and work best with a vest or cummerbund. Center vent, if any.

  Double-breasted jackets with peaked lapels should be worn with neither a vest nor a cummerbund. You ought to be younger than thirty-five and older than twenty-eight to wear one of these, and a perfect physical specimen. Fat guys, short guys, old guys beware. Double-breasted jackets with shawl collars are bizarre. Side vents, but ha! ha!

  Single-breasted jackets with a shawl collar should be worn only in the evening, if at all. No vents—or, if you need the air, a center vent.

- *Trousers:* These may have a small black strip of piping down the leg, but they won't have cuffs. Right?

- *Shirt:* Easy on big pleats and ruffles. Keep it simple; you don't want to look like a guy wearing a doily. The purpose of a tux is to make every guy look like every other guy so the women all look dazzling. Don't compete with the scenery, please.

- *Tie:* Black. Tie it yourself (see instructions later in this chapter).

- *Jewelry:* Black, gold, or silver studs, depending on the color of your watchband or eyeglasses. No other jewelry should be visible. That means no necklaces, please, lest somebody think you're King o' Porn or an off-duty sommelier.

- *Simple cummerbund* in black—or red, if you just have to be wild. A couple of ancillary cummerbund notes:
  Never wear a cummerbund with double-breasted formal wear.

Wear those cummerbund pleats up. (Long ago, men out on the town used to keep their tickets to the opera tucked in the pleats of their cummerbunds.)

- **Shoes:** Black patent-leather oxfords or pumps. Black tassel loafers with a high shine do fine.

HOW TO TIE A BLACK BOW TIE

The planet is increasingly a dress-down kind of place; you can wear your Silver Bullet windbreaker to church, or your Speedo to a bowling alley, and nobody'll pay much attention. Then comes June. Just as the weather starts to warm, the icy curtain of formal occasions rises. At weddings, receptions, parties, and graduations, guys who have been

clip-on cool all year long suddenly turn into loosely knotted nerds. Who would have ever thought it would be the job of *bow ties* to separate the men from the boys?

- *Warm up* by using your date's thigh as a temporary neck. Tie the necktie around the leg just as if you were tying your shoe, and you'll get the hang of the knot.
- *Neck it:* Drape the tie around your neck with one end hanging just slightly below the other.
- *Square:* Next, tie a simple square knot, the knot you were born knowing how to tie.
- *Pull the bows into shape* by tugging at them until they're arranged in the shape and pattern you want.
- *Three knot notes:*
  1. A black tie will have a smaller, tighter knot than a conventional bow tie.
  2. If you avoid looking in the mirror and just tie the damned thing as if you were trying your shoe, you may have better luck.
  3. A perfectly proportioned tie will have ends that stick out on the sides about as far as the ends of your jaw, but no farther.

How to Hold Up Your Trousers

Use belts and braces.

The old-fashioned kind of B & D is really the only one we ever understood. Yes, yes. You can dress up your wife in this stuff. But at a certain age, the belt looks better on you than it does on her.

Given its traditional use—separating your belly from your thighs—and considering a belt is sometimes all that stands between you and indecent exposure, it pays to know a good one from a bad one.

BRACING FOR BELTS

Braces are a bit pompous if worn ostentatiously, but any will do. Avoid clip-ons, though.

How to Drape a Torso

There are two kinds of shirts: dress shirts and all other shirts. What you wear off-duty is anybody's guess and nobody's concern. So let's rush through the notes we've got on fatigues first, and get down to business later.

BASIC T-SHIRT BASICS

There's a reason they're called "T-shirts" and not "tea shirts." We're talking underwear here, chaps. Far be it from me to defend the tattered flag of formality, but anybody who was irritated by Madonna's stage clothes during the late 1980s wasn't looking carefully at his own wardrobe.

- *The collar is the Main Thing* on a tee. You can tell by feel how thick and well-made a T-shirt collar is. As long as that stays together, the rest of the shirt can fall apart and you'll still look jake. But a shirt with great weave and a lousy, sagging, blown-out collar is a lousy shirt.

- *As undershirts.* Just because T-shirts are underwear doesn't mean you should actually wear them under anything. There's something about a T-shirt visible under a dress shirt that screams "Weenie" at the top of its lungs. Colored shirts are especially goofy looking under dress shirts. However, T-shirts can look fine under a casual shirt. But we're talking crew neck here. No V-necks no place.

An unconvincing dissent: A cotton undershirt worn under a dress shirt can help make the shirt last longer and look better. On a hot day, the added cotton keeps you cooler, believe it or not.

- *Long-sleeve mock turtleneck.* T-shirts look great under a blazer or jacket. They stay neat and trim and make your shoulders look wider than they really are. Color is a matter of preference.

An instant dissent: Turtlenecks of any kind, whether worn under jackets or not, are the rough above-the-waist equivalent of SansaBelt trousers. But if you're going to wear one, wear a good one—something made from cashmere or at least lamb's wool. A turtleneck under a jacket looks like lounge-lizard leisure wear, and if you have even a 5 percent body-fat problem, a snugly fitting knit shirt only provides cheap fabric for all that abdominal upholstery.

- *King-sized censor.* T-shirt lit is a colorful genre. But, a correspondent writes, "Can I ask other guys a favor? I have two little kids, just now getting to be able to read. If you wear a T-shirt with an obscenity on it, I see that the same as screaming cuss words at my wife and kids, and I'll object.

  "PS—I'm 6′3″ and I weigh 240."

WORK SHIRT WICK

If you really have to work for a living and you have to dress for work, work in a cotton shirt. Even the smallest amount of synthetic added to the weave will reduce cotton's natural ability to breathe efficiently and wick away moisture. Guys working in hot climates know that a heavy cotton shirt can provide a kind of wearable air-conditioning: The shirt works just like a swamp cooler.

HOW TO SHOOT A CUFF

Get this: Guy goes out, blows six hundred on a suit and twenty bucks on a shirt, then can't figure out why the suit looks so lousy.

If your dress shirt doesn't fit properly, all the effort you put into getting your suit tailored to fit you well will go to waste.

So here, well pressed and chock full o' starch, is what you need to know about dress shirts:

- *Buy dress shirts from a reputable maker.* Men don't like to shop around for shirts—or most other items of clothing. Once they find a good shirtmaker, they stick with the label. If they're let down even once, it's adios. Shirtmakers know this and mind their buttons and closures.
- *Buy your shirts in an exact size.* S-M-L-XL is too vague for grown-up shirt sizes. Even two-inch variables—16 by 32–34, for example—are the sure sign of a cut-rate shirt.
- *Get a fresh measurement every year.* This is because all things change, including you. Necks, especially, fluctuate. Your collar should fit snugly when buttoned—not so loose that your tie

hangs away from your neck, not so tight as to be pinching the skin. In fact, plastic surgeons are having a boom right now doing a new surgical procedure that takes away excess skin from the neck in men that is not naturally occurring, but the result of wearing a collar that is far too tight and has therefore stretched the skin of the neck for hours and hours each day.

- **Sleeve length:** The sleeve should end about five inches above the tip of the thumb. Another landmark: With a jacket on, your shirt's sleeve should extend about a half inch below the edge of your jacket cuff when your arm is at your side. More than an inch showing? Your jacket sleeve is going to look mighty short.

- **Fit.** Buy shirts that hang about six inches below your waist before you tuck them in. This extra length will be enough to stay tucked in without bulging around the midsection from the creep of excess fabric.

- **Cotton only.** Unless you're dressing for a novelty act, 100 percent cotton should be your only shirting choice. Why? Because a cotton shirt, well-pressed, well-laundered, perfectly sized, is one of the few things a man can wear that deserves the term "exquisite." Cotton is also the most comfortable shirting fabric.

- **Collars:** When you look at a shirt in a clothier's, you have to remember that when you put it on, your head and neck will be sticking out of the top. So remember to choose a collar that complements your head. If you have a short neck, get a collar that sits low. If you have a long neck, get a collar that is higher.

Collar rise: A good rule of thumb is that the collar should stand about a half inch above the back of your jacket collar. Look for stitching around the outer edges that makes the collar rigid. A well-made collar is less likely to sag and flatten with wear. Some of the more expensive shirts have hand-stitched collars. This stitching should always be subtle or almost invisible.

Closure: The two sides of the collar should *meet* at the neck and form a perfect V. Don't count on a necktie to bring the two together. Even a small gap—say a quarter inch—will make your shirt look like the ill-fitting, shabbily made thing it is. It'll also make your necktie look wonky.

Points: When you're wearing it, the points of the collar should touch the chest of the shirt. (See the discussion of types of collars, below.)

- ***Stitching:*** The better the shirt, the more stitches on the collar there will be per inch.
- ***Select the shirt to match the suit.*** To choose a shirt to go with a particular suit, consider the image the suit portrays. A casual tweedy or woolen suit calls for a casual button-down or rounded collar. A conservative pinstripe suit calls for a shirt with a stiffer collar with sharp points. Button-down collars are never appropriate as evening wear.

How to Dissect a Shirt

A good corporate soldier should be able to break down his shirt and reassemble it in thirty seconds under fire at a stockholders' meeting. Know the parts, know the shirt:

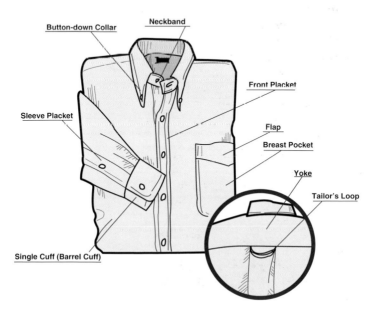

Button-down Collar
Neckband
Front Placket
Sleeve Placket
Flap
Breast Pocket
Yoke
Tailor's Loop
Single Cuff (Barrel Cuff)

- **Cuffs:** Pick one. Barrel? Or French?
  Barrel cuffs are those with one or two buttons and buttonholes.
  French cuffs are twice the length of a barrel cuff, and then folded in half over the outside of the shirt and held together with a cuff link.
- **Plackets:** The area of the shirt that the buttonholes are sewed into. In the good old days, the placket was a separate piece of fabric. Today, the placket is just simulated by folding the fabric of the shirt over. Plackets are generally an inch and a half wide.
- **The yoke** is a piece of fabric sewed across the back of the shirt, at the shoulders. It is used to attach the front and the back of the shirt together. An added touch is a split yoke, or a yoke for the back left and another for the back right, where both half-yokes are sewed together in the middle. A split yoke is a sign of quality. A bad yoke isn't funny. See?
- **A gauntlet** is the term for a sleeve placket, or that area of the shirt before the cuff where the sleeve is split. A higher-quality shirt will have a button on the gauntlet. Why add a gauntlet button? So you can close the gap when buttoning the sleeve of the shirt, and open the gap to roll up your sleeves when washing.

Neck Notes

The collar on a traditional dress shirt has regular points. Everything else is everything else:

- **Windsor collars** have points that are cut at a wider angle than the regular straight-point collar. They also sit lower, thus exposing more of the shirt at the neckline. The Windsor collar goes particularly well with double-breasted suits, but worn with more informal blazers or tweed jackets, it looks like a cheap shirt.
- **English spread collars** show more of the shirt at the neckline than the traditional dress-shirt collar and less than the Windsor. It is considered dressy while still giving an indication of the wearer's sense of style. Prince Charles and his pop are two fans of the English spread collar.
- **Pin collars:** These prissy jobs, with a pinhole on each side for a tie pin, are for men with longish necks.

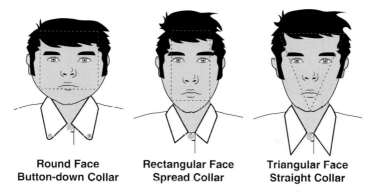

Round Face
Button-down Collar

Rectangular Face
Spread Collar

Triangular Face
Straight Collar

How to Collar Your Noggin: Straight collars are good for guys with oval or triangular faces. Spread collars are good for rectangular faces, but bad for round ones. Button-down collars work for everybody, but look best on round-faced men.

- *Tab collars* are much like pin collars, except they come with a snap or tab buckled behind the tie.
- *Rounded collars* are—well, *rounded*. These are as close to wearing a doily as most men can get while sober.

How to Iron a Shirt

Eight little steps to complete self-sufficiency:

1. **Start with a clean shirt,** something flat that resembles an ironing board, and an iron.
2. **Water it.** Get out a spray bottle or an old squirt gun and moisten the shirt.
3. **Begin with the collar.** Iron only the back, and iron it flat. Let your tie handle the job of putting in the fold. If you do it, it'll look squirrely.
4. **Next, iron the yoke** of the shirt. That's the part of the shirt that goes over your shoulders in the back. (See above.)
5. **Attack those sleeves.** If you like a crease, make sure you flatten the material out so that the crease on the shoulder matches the inside seam. The guys who work at expensive clothing stores will

tell you that a good shirt will never have a crease on the sleeve; if you buy their advice, you can forgo the crease by stuffing a towel inside the sleeve before ironing.

6. **Don't forget the placket on the sleeve**—that's the part of the sleeve where the button and buttonhole are. Technical term (as noted earlier): the gauntlet.

7. **Next, finish off the back** of the shirt, **then the front**—which is the most important part.

8. **Complete the job by ironing the placket** down the front of the shirt—get around those buttons good—and **then the cuffs.**

How to Ring a Neck

At least once a day, somewhere, somebody turns to a perfectly happy chappy and asks, "Hey, mister. Whatcha wearing a tie for?"

What in the name of heaven has caused this epidemic of informality? Since when do you treat life as though it were a big come-as-you-are party?

Like a simple suit, a necktie is a badge of honor, the battle ribbon of a veteran of the Great Game, the consolation prize of existence, the oriflamme of our gender. A reasonable necktie proclaims your seriousness about the business of being a man. Hang a necktie around your neck, and you're saying, "The Doctor Is In," you're saying, "Take a Number, Please," you're saying, "Do Not Talk to the Driver While the Bus Is in Motion." You're marking yourself as a man to be reckoned with.

THE LANGUAGE OF NECKTIES

A necktie is not a throwaway garment. As much as your suit, your shoes, and your shirt, a necktie makes a statement about you that is loud and clear. That's why a tie should be worn with the same insouciant sassiness normally associated with hats. A necktie has its own rakish tilt, its own dark threat, its own open innocence. A florid spectacle afloat on a sea of gray flannel can be worn only by men who are supremely confident of themselves.

But there are notable exceptions. And all of them are bow ties.

BOW TIES

For most men, formal occasions requiring formal dress provide sufficient justification to wear one of these poseur-ribbons. But prom night and the occasional wedding apparently aren't enough for those who aspire to a kind of daily vamp of poofy superciliousness. On a regular basis throughout this great nation, bow ties are worn everywhere by men who are both terrified and deeply affected.

Why? Who knows. Maybe it's because fifty, seventy-five years ago, bow ties were worn by radio wiseguys and newspaper columnists who traded barbed comments with good-looking dames across a round table. Now every jack with a bow around his neck thinks he's F. P. Adams. As the millennium pales, bow ties have gone one step beyond casual sassiness to something much more depraved: the empty emblem of eccentric cuteness. A bow tie apparently proclaims a man to be witty, brilliant, perhaps a chap of Thurberesque genius. The trouble is, so many men who wish to be seen as Thurberesque geniuses are now wearing bow ties that the claim of brilliance made by that cheap square of gaudy cloth obviously cannot possibly be universally true. Instead of smart men making witty remarks, all we have is a bunch of boring dorks wearing bow ties.

There are only two men in America who may wear bow ties as a badge of merit: George Will and Charles Osgood. Nobody else. All other bowtie guys are just faking wit. Failing to find a cute thing to say, they try instead for a cute thing to wear. And the very best they can come up with is a lousy bow tie.

What is being said of importance here is that if you wish to call attention to yourself, paint your face red and dye your hair blue, but don't get stupid with neckwear, since people looking at obnoxious men in silly ties see only a rope where the tie ought to be, and secretly they smile to themselves.

But if you must, here's how you tie one. Imagine your head is your shoe, and imagine your bow tie is your shoelace. Tie the tie the same way you'd tie your shoe. Stick out your tongue, if you have to. (See also above, under "How to Tie a Black Bow Tie.")

NEVER MIND THE QUALITY

Width

In the last twenty-five years, ties, like the men who have worn them, have put weight on and taken weight off. When JFK was president, cool guys wore skinny little exclamation points around their necks. By the time LBJ was out of there, ties were *five inches wide.* Good pilots could set an F-14 down on the neckties of the early 1970s. When God made the first tie, he made it three and one-half inches wide, and he condemned to perpetual ridicule anybody who wavered more than three-quarters of an inch either way. American-made box suits like those from Brooks Brothers and standard-issue neckwear are a timeless combo, the kind of thing that will do for a lifetime for those men who have no need to pursue late-breaking fashion.

A dissent: The cheapest, easiest way of making sure your wardrobe is up-to-date is to update your necktie collection on a regular basis. Don't throw away the old ones, though, since they'll be in fashion again within ten years.

Length

Ties vary in length, generally from fifty-four to fifty-eight inches, so it can be difficult to get one to land at the top of your belt buckle, as it should. Here's how to end that dilemma in your life, once and for all: Always take with you, when you go shopping for ties, one that you already have that is the right length.

KNOT NEGOTIABLE

There are three knots every self-respecting man ought to be able to tie before he dies: a square knot, a clove hitch, and a knot we can call *the Single* (or Half-) *Windsor.*

New tie knots show up from time to time, usually to accommodate some oddity in neckwear design. But the knot that most men use never changes, and they usually call it a "Windsor" of some sort, but it usually isn't. Whatever it is, however, it's the knot they live with, at least until the undertaker ties that loose confection called the Mortician Special.

The Knot to Know: The Single Windsor

Sometimes mistakenly called a "Half-Windsor," the SW is tied by simply passing the end of the tie beneath a first cross throw. It is a simple knot and it is superior to all others. The genius of this little tangle is that it allows for easy adjustment and, more important, for a balanced, well-proportioned knot. In a moment of feverish lust, it can be removed, completely untied, with one hand, and looped around a willing wrist in a nanosecond. Because the knot is so compressible, it can be used with ties of almost any fabric: Big, bulky ties can be made to look sleek with a smallish knot, while flimsy, silk flutterers can be given the substance of a larger knot. Properly tied, the Single Windsor will provide a small pleat just off-center and below the knot. A fabulous knot, and the result of Darwinianism, too: The Single Windsor is a more manageable version of a Double Windsor, the knot Laraine Day taught to Cary Grant in *Mr. Lucky* because the knot he'd been wearing was too goiteresque for a swell.

Are Knots Important?

As important as the tie they bind. The peculiar look some English people and some New Jersey automotive retailers bring to neckwear— with knots to the right and knots to the left and knots bulging beneath their throbbing ruby-red necks like smuggled grapefruit—is a result of overzealous neck tying, of throwing a Double Windsor into a tie that just can't stand that much complication. Most ties need only a simple knot firmly, but not tightly, wound, and centered close where the collar meets, with no shirt visible above.

Here's a rule of thumb: If your tie crisscrosses itself more than four times, total, you're a man with a neckwear problem—*knot*. And above all, the knot ought not be the focal point of the tie. When you look at a man's tie, your eyes should be drawn to a point approximately three inches *below* the knot, or about an inch below the point where the pleat stops.

How to Dress for Weather

OUTERWEAR

The Overcoat

Here is the Main Thing you need to know about this garment:

The overcoat is used primarily to fend off the cold when your suit jacket or blazer is not enough.

- *Color:* Black, navy, or camel.
- *Material:* Wool, cashmere, or camel.
- *Size:* Big enough to fit over a suit jacket or blazer, but not so large that it looks like you're camping in it for the night.
- *Length:* Sleeves should extend slightly past the shirt sleeves. Bottom should go well below the knees.
- *Style:* Overcoats are not a yearly renewable in the ecoforest of your wardrobe. Go for something traditional and, if you're over ninety, you'll wear the same overcoat for the rest of your life. Anything "fashionable" or trendy will make you look like a fool when next year's fashions and trends hit the street. Something simple, single-breasted, and without a belt (which you will lose) fits the traditional bill.

Another tip for keeping your overcoat for a long time: Avoid one that is fitted around the waist.

Trench Coat Dispatch

- *Color:* God intended all trench coats to be beige or tan.
- *Fabric:* High-quality woven cotton.
- *Style:* For once in your life, indulge yourself and pick out the same one that Bogey would have worn. You'll be glad you did. Gunflaps, belts, epaulets, and wristbands all serve a useful purpose: They keep out the wind and rain.
- *Lining:* Want a zip-out lining? Before you buy a coat with a removable lining, make sure the lining and zipper are well made, since this is where most of the wear and stress will occur. When you remove the lining, look for a strip of fabric inside the outer garment that will hide the zipper when you wear the shell without the lining.

Also, when you send the coat out to be cleaned, send the lining as a separate garment.

Jacket Copy

Like a hat or a pair of trousers, the jacket you wear should have some relationship to the body that's wearing it:

- *Short, heavy men* should wear longer jackets.
- *Short, slim men* should wear short jackets.
- *Tall, heavy men* should wear midlength jackets.
- *Tall, slender men* can wear anything they want.

Another jacket tip: Make sure you have enough room in a new jacket to move. Think of your jacket as the principal thing in your wardrobe when you want to dress up to catch a baseball or pick up a child or change a tire.

HOW TO LOOK CRISP ON A WILTING-HOT DAY

Nothing like a bracing dip in the swollen, wet heat of an August day in hell to make you realize that the difference between you and Jacques Cousteau is the accent. You know, it doesn't always have to be like this. You can go through life as a dry human being, a man with crisp pleats and an actual crease, a chap with a honker from which no drop of sweat ever drops. All you have to do is be cool and dress for hot.

Evaporation's the Main Thing

You need natural fibers, such as cotton, if you really want to wear cool clothing. Cotton allows air to pass through the weave, even as it seeks out the smallest possible pool of perspiration, wicks it away from the skin, and uses the moisture for air-conditioning.

Avoid Linen, Silk, and Wool

Linen is Hot! How it ever got a rep for being a cool, summer-weight fabric is a matter for the courts. As you perhaps already know from personal experience, not only is linen hot and ugly, it wrinkles pronto: Put on a crisp linen suit and in five minutes you'll look like Columbo's body double. Silk? Same deal. Wool? You bet; wool is for winter. Linen, silk, and wool all have tubular fibers that keep the fabric from breathing and lock in the heat your body produces. Linen and silk are

even worse than either one alone. Ironically, however, if you weave silk and wool together, you're okay.

HOW TO DRESS LIKE 007

Bond James Bond has the right idea when it comes to clothes: Quality counts; flamboyance and flashiness don't. Here's the generic breakdown on zip-zip-seven's wardrobe:

- **Suit:** Standard issue, dark blue. Look to the weather to be your guide, but when it comes to fabric you only have three choices: serge, alpaca, or tropical worsted.
- **Shirt:** White, cotton, grabber collar—that is, a collar with a pin, tab, or other device to keep the points down.
- **Socks:** Very dark blue.
- **Tie:** Dark, knit, silk. And there's only one Bond knot: a regular-round-over-and-through—a.k.a. a Single Windsor.
- **Shoes:** Plain black. Moccasins for ease of movement, maybe? Well polished.

What does all this tell you? Next to attitude, wardrobe means nothing

How to Become an Optical Illusion

The magnificent six: "Oh, no!" you say to yourself, "time to either get myself in shape or get my wardrobe in shape." We know the answer. Here are a half-dozen ways to help you *look* thinner than you really are:

1. *Breathe.* Wear a shirt with a collar that's not squeezing that extra chin up and out of your throat. Pointed collars make your chin look longer.
2. *Wear a loose-fitting jacket* with shoulders wider than your hips.
3. *Subdue!* Avoid eye-grabbing neckties.
4. *Choose a fabric that drapes smoothly.* Gabardines and worsteds are good.
5. *Use a conventional-width cuff.* Anything between an inch and an inch and a half will do.
6. *Shine your shoes.* Or, if they're wide and thick-soled, toss 'em in favor of a new pair with a thin sole.

HOW TO DRESS A FOOT FOR WORK

Real-life conversation:

First chap: "The guy from Harvard, did he get the job?"

Second chap: "You kidding? Did you see those *shoes*?"

The lesson: When it comes to sizing you up, you just never know how low a guy will go. Sometimes, out of the whole cosmic soup of a wardrobe, the last thing ends up being the **Main Thing.**

The Seven Sole Sisters

1. *The plain cap-toe* and the perforated cap-toe. These are the dressiest business shoes money can buy. They come in black and various shades of brown, and they are the staple of the business world. They are only appropriate with business wear, particularly of worsted wool and flannel. Ironically, these shoes were originally designed for men in the military.

2. **Wing tips:** In the world of business, they come in just three colors: black, brown, cordovan. Because of the additional detail, they can be worn with textured fabrics like tweeds and cheviots, as well as worsteds and flannels.

3. **Slip-ons,** or dress loafers: Go easy on the giant, flapping chunks of metal. You could hurt somebody.

4. **The monk strap:** Plain-toed, with a buckle on the side, it allows the wearer to show a bit of style beyond traditional foot wear. The classic version is made of suede and was originated by the church.

5. **Suede shoes:** Originally intended only to be worn in the English countryside. If your business environment will let you get away

Men's shoes Top: monk strap, wingtip, cap toe. Second: tassel loafer, suede shoes, loafer. Bottom: Topsider-type boating shoe.

with it, these shoes look great with a casual suit and even better, in contrast, with more severe and conservative suits.

6. *The tassel loafer:* Originally thought to be unacceptable for business, but that thinking has changed in some circles. Here's a rule of thumb: If a blue blazer isn't dressy enough for where you are going, this shoe isn't either. Be careful your tassel is reasonable. If it looks like you mugged a stripper for footwear, you've gone too far.

7. *Summer shoes:* These shoes are for men who can't bear to wear the same style year-round. Essentially, summer shoes are shoes in colors lighter than black, brown, and cordovan to go with lighter-colored summer suits.

Technical data: For business shoes, the soles should be a quarter-inch thick or less. The job of the sole is to protect your feet and give support. Heels should be low and follow the line of the shoe. Both should be close-clipped to the rest of the shoe. The welt is what the sole is attached to; a fine pair of shoes will use stitching. The vamp is the leather part of the shoe that covers the top of the foot; a low vamp makes for a sleeker looking shoe.

HOW TO SHOP FOR SHOES

- *Wait until later* in the day, when your feet have had a chance to swell to their largest size.
- *Wear the same socks* you will be wearing when you wear the shoes you are about to buy.
- *Break:* It may be helpful to also wear the type of trousers you will be wearing the shoes with, to see how they will look in action.

HOW TO TAKE CARE OF YOUR SHOES

Get into the habit of having your shoes repaired regularly. Your shoes will last longer for two reasons: First, they will never get run down to the point where the repair is pointless. Second, your shoe repair man will get to know you and take better care of you. Other wing tips:

- *Polish your shoes before you wear them* for the first time. This will help them stay clean and maintain a good coat of polish.

How to Cover Your Other End: Hats you've heard of, caps you love. From most formal to least:
Top: Top hat, hamburg, cowboy
Second: Fedora, boater, derby
Third: Eight- and six-part caps, seamed cap
Fourth: Flat-top, Fudd-the-hunter, fur cap (Detroit shape)
Bottom: Standard American ball cap

- ***Don't wear the same pair*** of shoes two days in a row. Let them rest, air out, snap back into shape between wearings.
- ***Keep your heels in good repair.*** Wearing shoes with worn heels causes the leather to stretch in ways that it shouldn't.

- ***Polish shoes often*** to keep the leather fresh.
- ***Keep shoe trees in shoes*** to help them retain their shape.
- ***Clean suede shoes*** with a suede brush or an artist's gum eraser.

Banana spit: Great execs know time is money. If you're in need of a quick shine, but don't have the time to find a can of polish, try this time-tested ploy: Go to the zoo. Visit the monkeys. Take off all your clothes and sneak into the monkey cage. When some baboon isn't looking, swipe his banana. Climb out, get dressed, knock the dust off your shoes, then rub your leather uppers with the inside of the banana peel. Remove any particles left behind. Then give the shoe a good buff with a napkin. Now you're ready to make ***decisions.***

How to Shop for Blue Jeans

In retail, there's a confusing helix of jeans, with prices ranging into serious three-digits for what are supposed to be rough work trousers. But when it comes time to dress-down, don't dumb-down for the occasion. Simply follow this **Main Thing** rule: *It's unnecessary for any pair of blue jeans to cost more than a pair of Levi's 501s.*

It's not that other jeans might not look better on a chap than a pair of standard-issues; 501s look especially weird on some bodies. It's just that there's no reason for anybody to need to charge more for theirs than Levi Strauss does. You can't get better denim, and you can't get better manufacturing. So no matter how many years have passed since this book's first appearance, to find the very latest going price on a good pair of jeans, price a pair of 501s and go from there.

3. Fitness, Health, and Grooming

Once upon a time, the men women admired the most were fat Ottoman Turks, huge guys with beer guts and a swarm of dependents crammed into a seraglio someplace guarded by a bunch of thin, lithe eunuchs. No more. Now women like guys who look like the eunuchs, so it's good-bye big belly, and hello Tony Little.

The benefit of this, of course, is that we're leaner, meaner, and healthier men-machines. Why? Because we learned the little secret disclosed below—and behind a million magazine coverlines:

How to Get Fit Fast!

This little instruction is a dual **Main-Thing,** two-step gem:

1. Eat less.
2. Exercise more.

There are, however, some really ugly details, from food to fitness. We'll cover them all.

THE FOUR ROADS TO SWEAT

There are *four basic types of exercises.* Since most men don't have a whole lot of time for exercise, anyway, it's smart to choose a type of exercise that goes directly to your least favorite problem:

1. *Aerobics.* Great for cardio-circulatory strength. Pretty good at stretching and increasing metabolic rates. Lousy at muscle building.
2. *Endurance exercise.* The goal of an endurance routine is to get organs like your heart and lungs and other muscles to be able to work for longer and longer periods of time. An endurance exercise can be anything you do from running to walking to racquetball. Each specific activity will deliver its own virtue, but the point of an endurance exercise is to simply increase stamina.
3. *Strength training.* Building muscles can be more than just piling a heap o' bicep onto your upper arm. You can also strengthen things like your back and feel better for it.
4. *Flexibility exercise.* Yoga with a dash of anger. The emphasis in flex exercises is to loosen joints and tone muscles.

GETTING STARTED

The most important thing is simply realizing that not only can't you be lazy, you actually have to look for ways to be active. Try these, for starters:

- *Park a few blocks from work,* walk the rest of the way. And when you walk, try to be conscious of the exercise you're getting. Feel the strength in your legs, loosen your back as you go. Swing your arms freely. Feels good.

- *Take the stairs,* instead of the elevator.
- *Use your feet instead of the phone.* When you need to talk to someone down the hall or on another floor, go there. You might walk a few miles every day doing this alone.
- *Leave your car at the office* or in the garage and walk when you can.
- *Take the dog for a walk.*
- *Take the Significant Other for a walk.*
- *Turn off the TV* and the computer games and play a game outside with your kids.
- *Make two trips.* Forget efficiency. Whenever you have to get multiple items from one place to another, thumb your nose at time-saving techniques and deliberately carry one thing at a time.
- *Go to the grocery store with your wife.* Push the cart. Carry the groceries to the car one or two bags at a time. Make multiple trips with them into the house, as well. Your wife will think you're a gent. You'll think you're getting exercise. Only one of you will be right.
- *Let older neighbors know you are available* for carrying things like groceries and taking out the garbage. No, don't drive over there when they need help—start your workout by walking there.

HOW MUCH EXERCISE DO YOU NEED?

At a minimum, work out three times a week, for at least twenty minutes per workout.

How long should you exercise? For however long it takes.

HOW TO WARM UP

In many ways, *all the stuff you do before you do the hard part of any exercise or workout is the stuff that counts most.* You have to steadily increase your heart rate in preparation for a long-term exercise session, and you have to stretch your muscles so they don't tear with the exertion of whatever you're going to do next.

HOW TO STRETCH

Be careful, lads. *The two biggest candidates for injury are those who stretch too little and those who stretch too much.*

One stretch to avoid: the old toe-on-a-step-and-the-back-of-the-foot-hangs-off stretch. When you drop your weight down to stretch your calf muscle, you run the risk of overstretching both the calf and the Achilles.

Here is a list of great stretches:

- **Calf stretch.** This stretch treats one leg at a time. Take your time. Stand with one foot in front of another, about two to three feet from a wall. Your back leg should be straight, your front leg should be bent, and both feet should face the wall. Your hands are against the wall. Hold this position for ten seconds, then switch legs. Do this ten times.

- **Hamstring stretch.** Straighten one leg out in front of you and rest it on a footstool, with your knee locked. Bend at the waist and try to touch your head to your leg. Hold for ten seconds. Switch legs and repeat. Repeat ten times. Don't bob and bounce. Take it slow and easy and make all your movements smooth as peanut butter.

- **Knee and lower back.** Lie on the ground. Bring both knees to your chest. Hold for ten seconds. Repeat five times.

- **Push-up.** Come on. You know how to do this. Lie on the ground. Put your hands flat on the floor below your chest. Raise yourself by pushing up with your arms. Hold for ten seconds. Repeat five times.

- **Backward bend.** Stand straight. Put the palms of your hands against the small of your back. Tighten the muscles in your butt and bend backward. Hold for ten seconds, then relax. Repeat five times.

- **Skin stretch.** Sit on a clifftop with your legs hanging over the side. A table will also work. Put a light weight—say three, maybe five pounds—on your toes. Like, maybe a lightweight brass bell. Joke. Okay. Raise your foot at the ankle. Hold for six seconds. Repeat five times.

HOW TO RUN AROUND

You think about running and you think about a million long-stride steps between you and fitness. In reality, if you want to start running, there are only three steps, and they're all quite small:

Warm Up

Don't leave home without a decent stretch. And don't start stretching until you've loosened up a bit. A short walk will help, along with some twisting and bending exercises. Want the full limber-lore rundown? See earlier mention, under "How to Warm Up."

Run

When you run, run easy. The secret: You want to sweat, you want to get your heart beating, but you want to do it without bringing yourself to the point of heavy-breathing, Darth Vader-like exhaustion.

- *The ideal pace:* You'll know it when you find it. It'll be comfortable, and not something that will have you huffing and puffing. Try whistling a few bars of "It's a Small World, After All." If you can't, then either you're running too fast, or you've never been to Disneyland.

- *When you start,* run at least three times a week but not more than four. Make each run last at least twenty minutes; twenty minutes is what it takes to get your heart pounding, your lungs pumping, your glands sweating. And that twenty minutes doesn't include the time it takes you to warm up and cool down. It only includes the hard part.

- *Be a train. Run on time.* It's important to be consistent in scheduling your runs when you first start out. For instance, if you run

every other day for three weeks, and then you run three days in a row, and then you skip the next four days, you're only making things hard on yourself. The best thing to do is to schedule your running dates and times on your calendar and keep to the schedule.

IF YOU'VE NEVER RUN BEFORE
Begin by walking. Stretch your arms and legs out in front of you as you go.

TOE AND HEEL

Put some spring in your step. Sometimes, the world passes you by. Here's how to catch up:

- *Saunter:* The speed of the average person ambling over to the office watercooler is twenty minutes per mile (m/m), or three mph.
- *Stroll:* Your basic boulevard walker—a guy on his way to a job he enjoys, for example—is fifteen m/m or four mph.
- *Hell-on-leather:* A man with a mission—arms flying, heel-and-toe, and lapping the field—is cruising at a pace of 12 m/m. Figure five mph.
- *City speed:* Midtown Manhattan traffic at rush hour moves at two to three mph. On a Manhattan avenue, there are approximately twenty blocks per mile. The moral: You can hoof it to work faster than a cabbie can floor it. The benefit: A wonderful aerobic workout, especially on a fine, spring morning.
- *Next, jog slowly.* Despite its speedy rep, a jog is more of a fast walk than a slow run. Step on your heels, not on your toes, and rock as you would if you were walking at a normal pace. If you can't carry on a conversation as you jog, you're going too fast.
- *Speed it up.* When you feel comfortable at a jogger's pace, try running a bit. The difference between running and jogging or walking has as much to do with speed as it does with how your feet hit the ground and how long they stay there. Try it, come on. Stand up. When you walk, you put one foot down before you pick the other up. Right? See? Down. Up. Down. Up. When you run, you are pushing off with one foot as you place the other. If you try walking that way, you'll run.

- Over time, increase the amount of time in a workout you spend running *versus* jogging or walking.

Cool Down

When you are tired out from running, return to a jog—or, if it's more comfortable, return to a walk.

After your run, repeat some or all of your stretches.

After cooling down, lie on the ground or grass and stare at the sky for a short breather. Some guys pray. Some guys don't have a prayer, so they meditate.

First Step, Second Step

Next day: The hardest part of starting to run isn't doing it the first time. It's doing it the second time. Therefore, if you make it your goal to continue running on a regular schedule for, say, *four weeks,* it will be a lot easier for you to slip into your sneakers as part of a routine, rather than a one-time, two-time thing. Why? Because, you reason, anything as unpleasant as the first run just has to get easier. That isn't true, of course, until the tenth, or twentieth run, but at least you can see the top of the hill, after which everything is gravity-fed.

- *Madness:* Some people discover the feeling of joy in running. They are insane, of course. But it is possible to get to the point where you would miss it if you stopped running.

How to Tell Where You Stand

The difference between a beginner, intermediate, and advanced runner is this:

- *A beginner* will only be able to run a very small part of a twenty-minute workout. In some cases, the amount of time spent running will be only a few minutes, while the remainder of the time is spent walking or jogging.
- *An intermediate runner* will be able to run for twenty or thirty minutes without having to jog or walk.
- *An advanced runner* can run for thirty minutes or more without having to walk or jog. Marathon runners can go forever, which is why they are loved by all women.

HOW TO RIG A BARE-BONES GYM

All You Really Need

If you've got more ambition than bucks, here's the get-by, two-part minimum for putting together a workout facility designed primarily to raise your body's metabolism:

- *Sneakers*
- *Jump rope*

That's it. Everything else is optional. Run and skip your way to boy-god-hood.

Ten minutes with a jump rope is worth two days in the sack with Jessica Alba, if burning fat is what you're after.

Cinder blocks in various sizes, some two-by-fours, and a pulley are all you need to rig a cut-rate, cutthroat lifting station.

Add-ons

If money means nothing, add

- *A cross-country skiing machine or a treadmill*
- *A rowing machine*

Multifunctional, Nautilus-type equipment is nice, but not essential.

- *A set of weights.* Building muscles is an excellent way to really pump up your body's metabolic rate. Also, muscles eat calories *alive.*

HOW TO SPEND A LOT OF MONEY GETTING FIT

Join a health club. Talk about money! And if you're like most guys who join, check out the babes, give it a shot for a few weeks, then disappear, you might as well buy a self-help diet book you can ignore after a week. It would be a hell of a lot cheaper. Still, there *are* some valid reasons for joining a gym:

- *Camaraderie.* Sign up with a bud. The chances of slacking off are halved. Besides, it's more fun.
- *Instruction.* Most gyms have a trainer or therapist handy.
- *Tools.* Make sure the gym has a full range of equipment and services. Whatever it has, it's likely to be better equipment than most of us can afford.

HOW TO GET TO BUFF FROM FLAB IN A FLASH

Life is short. That's the really bad news. The good news is your list of essential exercises—the ones you really have to do if the object of your game is keeping your belly off your belt—is also short. There are exercise freaks out there, of course. But face it, you can exercise all day long and go from buff to more buff, but then you die fit and you miss life along the way.

The better bet: Figure out what part of your body needs fitness first aid, then focus on it. Here's your list:

How to Lose Weight Watching *The Office*: Run, and keep going.

THE MAIN-THING EXERCISE FOR EACH BROKEN-DOWN BODY PART

BODY PART	NO-FAIL EXERCISE *(FOR EACH OF THESE, START WITH EIGHT REPS AND GO FROM THERE.)*
Legs	**The squat.** Start with your feet slightly apart and a barbell across the back of your shoulders. Now, hunker down, duck-style, like a bear in the woods, until your thighs are parallel to the floor, then slowly raise up.
Calves	**Calf raise.** Grab a dumbbell and hold it in your left hand, arm down, palm facing in. Step onto a riser—a crate or a small bench, maybe, or something else that's at least six inches high. Stick your right foot behind your left heel and rise up on the toes of your left foot.

Don't take a tumble; you can use your right hand to brace yourself against a wall or a girlfriend. Next, lower yourself until your heel is a couple of inches below the top of the box. Do this eight times, then do it again with your right leg, and the dumbbell in your right hand. Own.

Butt	**Kneeling back kick.** Climb up on the end of a workout bench, grasping the sides. Hug it like you love it. Next, raise and extend your right leg directly behind you, until your foot is a few inches higher than your butt. Lower it back down to the bench, and repeat it seven more times, then switch to your other leg.
Chest	**Bench press.** Lying faceup on an exercise bench, grip a barbell with your hands slightly more than shoulder-width apart. Lower the bar slowly until it touches your chest. Leave it there. No, no! Just kidding. Slowly raise it back up. Eight reps.
Back	**Seated row.** You need a machine with a low pulley bar for this one. Sit on the floor in front of the bar, bend your knees a little, then reach out and grab the pulley bar with both hands. Pull it slowly to your chest, keeping your back straight and—as much as possible perpendicular to the floor throughout the movement.
Shoulders	**Military press.** Ten-hut, para jocks. Stand up or sit on an exercise bench. Grasp a barbell with your hands slightly farther than your shoulders. Raise the 'bell above your head, then lower it until it touches the back of your shoulders.
Triceps	**Triceps pushdowns.** Grab hold of a bar attached to a high-pulley cable. With your hands about six inches apart and with your elbows against your sides, bring the bar down until your forearms are parallel to the floor. That's where you start. Now, push the bar down until your arms are fully extended. Return to the starting point.
Biceps	**Dumbbell preacher curl.** You need the preacher curl station of your multi- for this one. Rest your upper arms on the pad, palms up. Curl the dumbbells up to your shoulders and down again slowly.

BODY PART	NO-FAIL EXERCISE
	(FOR EACH OF THESE, START WITH EIGHT REPS AND GO FROM THERE.)
Abdominals	*Belly-sag* is a four-exercise problem. The best of these is the classic crunch, below, but the others can also help big-time.

- **Crunch.** On your back, with your knees bent, feet together and about a foot from your rump. Cross your arms comfortably over your chest and curl your body upward until your shoulders are maybe six inches off the carpet. Stay there for a sec. Feel that burn? Good. Back down slow and easy.
- **Twisting crunch.** On your back, with your knees bent, feet together and about a foot from your rump. Cross your arms comfortably over your chest and curl your left shoulder toward your right knee until your left shoulder blade comes off the floor. Then come back down slowly and repeat from the other side. Remember to freeze for a couple of seconds at the top of each rep.
- **Seated barbell twist.** Sitting on the end of an exercise bench, place a barbell across the back of your shoulders. Keep your lower body facing forward and twist your torso to the left, back to the center, to the right, and then back again.
- **Side bend.** Stand with a dumbbell in your right hand. With your back straight, slowly bend to the right as far as possible. Return to the starting point and bend to your left. Do this eight times, then switch sides.

Noggin	See the section "How to Get Brain Buff" in chapter 7.

How to Carry Your Own Weight

Metaphorically, this would be a **Main Thing** to know. But we're dealing with the literal side of life in this chapter. Alas.

- *First, don't rush.* Position yourself close to the thing you want to lift.
- *Keep your feet shoulder-width apart.*
- *Bend at the knees*—not the waist.
- *Tighten your stomach muscles* as you lift to relieve the pressure on your lower back.
- *Never twist* your body while carrying a heavy load. Okay. Now you're fit. So let's get *crazy.*

HOW TO GET PSYCHO-FIT

If getting fit, to you, is more than just an extension of lifestyle eccentricities, more than just a subject of sweaty fanaticism, you'll be pleased to note that there's a guy out there who agrees with you. He's the guy who thought up what he calls "psycho-training," in which you die looking your best. Here, for the edification of us all, is how health clubs in America might operate if we handed over our towels and locker keys to North Koreans.

The Bifurcated Buffer

According to our correspondent, there are two parts to the psycho-trainer method of getting really huge really quickly:

1. **A sadistic partner.**
2. **Some sadistic exercise methods.**

Make no mistake about it, this workout is going to hurt, and it will hurt a lot. This is a good thing.

Pain Counts

Just lifting more is not enough to be psycho. You need to go for the big hurt. This can be achieved by upping the intensity of each exercise. There are two recommended ways for reaching psycho-intensity levels: preexhaustion and breakdown.

PREEXHAUSTION

This technique works well on complex exercises like the bench press and the military press. Let's look at the bench press:

- *Warm up.*

- **Get dumbbells** that you would normally use for flat-bench dumbbell flys. Know what a flat-bench dumbbell fly is? You lie on your back, dumbbell in each hand, your arms out on each side. Now squeeze your arms together back up at the top. After a while, it hurts good. Try it with about 40 pounds and see what happens. That's a "flat-bench dumbbell fly." Now ratchet it up to psycho-level:

- **Load the bench press** with slightly more than warm-up weight—maybe 150 pounds. With the 40-pound weights, do a set of dumbbell flys until you fail, and fail hard—but do at least twelve reps.

- **When you finally flag,** *immediately* drop the weights and start bench-pressing the 150-pound weight. This will suck and hurt. This is good. This is great for developing the chest, especially when the shoulders and arms are already tired from the week's previous workouts.

Preexhaustion uses an isolation exercise—the flys—to fatigue the chest to failure, then uses the relatively fresh shoulders and arms to force even more stress on the chest during the bench press. This is also a great exercise for those guys who fear they may die of heart failure at an early age, because they find out *right away* whether their fear has any basis in fact.

BREAKDOWN

The breakdown is a great way to increase the intensity and can be used on almost any exercise. It is generally best used in conjunction with your normal workout.

- **Go back** to the bench press.
- **Warm up.**
- **After a few sets** of your normal routine, load about 90 percent of your max onto the bench, or about what you can do for, say, two unassisted reps. Bench-press the weight for *four* reps, getting help as you need it from your sadistic spotter, who should note that the lifter should be just about purple by the time the weight gets back on the rack.
- **After putting the weight on the rack,** *immediately* strip off about 60 percent of it and keep benching, getting at least eight reps.

You need to strip off a good chunk of weight to make this principle work. If you are benching 150 pounds, fail hard, and then pull off only 20 pounds, the weight isn't going to feel any lighter, and you'll never be able to get the reps that you need.

- *In the last stage of a breakdown,* you should be able to bench at least six reps unassisted to make it work. The psycho-partner is very important in the last stage of the breakdown lift. The weight is light, but the lifter is tired. The partner uses psycho principles to focus the lifter's effort on lifting and get his mind off the awesome hurt he's feeling (he's doing it right). Two breakdown sets per exercise are usually enough.

Frequency

Three psycho-days per week of weights is enough. More will get you less. *Lifting seven days a week like a psycho is too much stress for your body to handle.* You will work yourself into a bad cycle of overtraining, in which you actually see negative results.

Harder, not longer, is the goal of these workouts. Doing a bazillion sets of an exercise may make you better at that exercise, but not improve the body part as much as doing fewer and harder sets. *Psycho-training should be used in conjunction with sensible planning.* Train psycho for a week, and use your normal training routine for a week, or alternate psycho and normal workouts. As always, let your body be the guide.

Rest is key. The body can't heal the massive amounts of stress you've placed upon it in a single day. In fact, sometimes it will take two or three days to fully recover.

The following are a couple of sample workouts and ways to divide your body up to maximize the psycho principles. These are general workouts and can be modified to suit your tastes. Remember, superior effort brings superior results. Get psycho and have fun. Or die.

Psycho-Workout Plan 1

The principle here is to go for more weight and fewer reps and the sets will progress. In psycho-training, eight to four reps at 60 to 80 percent of max is your standard coed stuff.

MONDAY: CHEST AND BACK

- *Bench press:* Three sets of eight to four reps, 60 to 80 percent of max. Two of the previous sets should combine preexhaustion and breakdown (as specified in the previous section).
- *Incline bench press:* Three sets of four to twelve reps, 50 to 100 percent of max.
- *Lat pulldowns.* Three sets of twelve to four reps, 50 to 80 percent of max. Two sets of breakdowns.
- *Cable rows:* Three sets of four to twelve reps, 50 to 80 percent of max. Two sets of breakdowns, from 90 percent to 60 percent of max. One set double breakdowns—fail, drop 60 percent, fail, drop 60 percent.

WEDNESDAY: SHOULDERS AND LEGS

- *Hack squats:* Three sets of fifteen to eight reps, 50 to 80 percent of max. *Then* one set of thirty-plus reps with warm-up weight.
- *Leg curls:* Three sets of twelve to eight reps, 50 to 80 percent of max.
- *Leg extensions:* Three sets of twelve to eight reps, 50 to 80 percent of max.
- *Military press:* Five sets of twelve to eight reps, 50 to 80 percent of max. Three sets preexhaustion using lateral dumbbell raises first.
- *Shoulder shrugs:* Two sets, 50 to 90 percent of max. Two sets double breakdowns. Ten to four reps.
- *Calf raises:* Three sets of ten to twenty reps, 50 to 90 percent of max; breakdowns on all sets.

FRIDAY: ARMS

- *Preacher bench curls:* Three sets of fifteen to eight reps, 50 to 80 percent of max.
- *Straight bar curls:* Three sets, all breakdowns.
- *Concentration curls:* Two sets of *double* breakdowns.
- *Lying French presses* (skullcrushers): One set normal of fifteen to eight reps, 50 to 80 percent of max. Two sets of breakdowns.
- *Triceps pushdowns:* Two sets normal of fifteen to six reps, 50 to 80 percent of max.

- *Triceps kickbacks:* Three sets of twelve to ten reps, *with good form.*

Psycho-Workout Plan 2

MONDAY: CHEST AND BACK

- *Bench press:* Three sets with preexhaustion and breakdown (as specified above).
- *Incline bench press:* Three sets of four to twelve reps, 50 to 100 percent of max; breakdowns on all sets.
- *Lat pulldowns:* Two sets of twelve reps at 50 percent of max, four reps at 80 percent of max. *Then* do a breakdown immediately after the last set at 80 percent.
- *Dead lifts:* Two sets of fifteen to ten slow reps (two to four seconds up and two to four seconds down).

WEDNESDAY: SHOULDERS AND LEGS

- *Squats:* Three sets of fifteen to thirty reps, 50 to 80 percent of max.
- *Leg curls:* Two sets of twelve to eight reps, 50 to 80 percent of max.
- *Leg extensions:* Two sets of twelve to eight reps, 50 to 80 percent of max.

- *Military press:* Three sets of twelve to eight reps, 50 to 80 percent of max. Two sets preexhaustion using lateral dumbbell raises first.
- *Shoulder shrugs:* Two sets, 50 to 90 percent of max. Two sets double breakdowns.
- *Calf raises:* Three sets of ten to twenty reps, 50 to 90 percent of max. Toes in and out on at least two of the sets.

FRIDAY: ARMS
- One sixty-second slo-mo chin-up (thirty seconds up, thirty seconds down), followed by straight bar curls (eight to twelve reps). Do this cycle twice. Then:
- *Concentration curls:* Two sets of double breakdowns.
- One sixty-second slow-mo dip (thirty seconds up, 30 seconds down), followed by *lying French presses* (skullcrushers). Do this cycle twice.
- *Triceps pushdowns:* Two sets normal of fifteen to six reps, 50 to 80 percent of max.
- *Triceps kickbacks:* One set of ten to twelve reps, *with good form.* You are now psycho fit.

Health

There's only one **Main** health-related **Thing** we all want to know:

How to Live Forever

Never get sick. On the other hand, there's nothing like a bout of acute hypochondria to put the fear of God into an otherwise healthy man.

THE HYPOCHONDRIA CHECKLIST

Feeling lousy? Like there's some ugly tumor growing just inside your forehead? Could be brain cancer. Or it could be hypochondria. Here's how to tell the difference:

1. When your doctor makes a diagnosis, do you feel it's probably wrong?

2. After you read or hear about a new illness or disease, do you find that the symptoms describe what you're suffering?
3. Have you ever gone from doctor to doctor because you felt your old one wasn't taking you—and your grotesque illnesses—seriously enough?
4. If you asked your friends how often you talk about your health, would they laugh out loud?
5. Do you feel sick if your doctor discovers that what ails you is really some thing very much less significant than the ebola variant you had imagined?
6. Are you often on the phone with your doctor to describe new symptoms of new illnesses?
7. Did you answer yes to one or more of the above? If so, the next illness you talk to your doctor about ought to be hypochondria. The nice thing is, this time the doctor's bound to listen and be enthusiastic about helping, and also have plenty of experience with your problem. Hypochondria afflicts as many as half of all visitors to a typical family doctor's office.

DEATH'S DIRTY DOZEN

On the other hand, here are the actuarial all-stars, the twelve—okay, eleven—horses upon which the grim reaper rides. Say hello now. You may become better acquainted later.

Although, note: *Mike Lafavore once told me that if science discovered tomorrow the magic bullet that could cure all known cancers, our average lifespan would increase just slightly more than two years. But if science found a cure for all forms of heart disease tomorrow, we'd all get an extra decade or more.*

1. *Heart disease/heart attack*
   Symptoms: Intense pain in the chest, feels like a heaviness or intense pressure. It may extend beyond your chest into your left shoulder and arm or into both arms, or to your back, neck, teeth, and jaw. At first it may feel like intense indigestion and may be accompanied by nausea, vomiting, a shortness of breath, and intense bouts of sweating.

2. *High blood pressure/hypertension*

   Symptoms: No outward symptoms, but if you have a family history of hypertension, eat a lot of salt, drink a lot, are obese, are African-American, get little or no exercise, have problems sleeping, or are often stressed out, you are a good candidate.

3. *Prostate cancer and prostatitis*

   Symptoms of prostate cancer: Problems urinating, which include an inability to urinate or start urinating, blood in the urine, a weak or interrupted flow, a flow that is painful to stop, burning sensations when urinating. Increased need to urinate at night. Lower back pain, and pain in the upper thighs and pelvis.

   Symptoms of prostatitis: Fever, problems (burning, bleeding) urinating, lower back pain, pain in the upper thighs and pelvis.

   The two illnesses aren't the same thing. Both are painful, but while prostate cancer can kill you, prostatitis hurts more. While some researchers have suggested hormonal imbalance or immune system disorders as causes for prostatitis, the chances are it's a bacterial or viral illness. Doctors aren't sure yet, since they can't find a specific infection in most sufferers, but the routine prescription is for antibiotics, since that's what seems to work best.

   Guys over forty ought to get to know their doctors on this one: A yearly checkup—called, with delicate poetry, a "digital-rectal exam"—is mandatory for midlife men. Besides, the self-exams are a pain.

   Five wisecracks every urologist loves to hear: Does this mean we have a relationship? I suppose now you've lost all respect for me. I know you: You won't even call me tomorrow. We never talk.

4. *Diabetes*

   Symptoms of insulin-dependent diabetes: Frequent urination, sudden weight loss, excessive thirst and hunger, weakness, fatigue, irrational behavior or irritability, nausea, vomiting.

5. *Stroke*

   Symptoms: A sudden feeling of weakness on one side of the body—in the face, or on the hand, arm, or leg; loss of speaking ability or loss of the ability to understand what others are saying; double vision, loss of vision in one eye or a dimming of vision in one eye; headaches without a cause or a change in a normal pattern of headaches;

dizziness, vertigo, unsteadiness, proneness to falling; an awkwardness or clumsiness with one limb or more—a symptom which may first be detected as an unexplained change in handwriting.

6. *Emphysema*
   Symptoms: Shortness of breath; chronic, persistent, often mild cough.

7. *Lung cancer*
   Symptoms: Persistent coughing that contains phlegm, which may be blood-streaked. Shortness of breath, chest pain, hoarseness, loss of appetite, loss of weight.

8. *Pneumonia*
   Symptoms: Painful cough with or without bloody phlegm, pain in the chest, difficulty breathing, fatigue, chills, high fever.

9. *Tuberculosis*
   Symptoms: Begins with mild cough and fever; followed by chronic fatigue. Also, weight loss, cough with bloody phlegm, fever, and night sweats.

10. *Liver disease and cirrhosis*
    Symptoms: Loss of appetite and/or weight loss, nausea and vomiting, fatigue, weakness, jaundice, pain in the abdomen and intestinal bleeding, easy bruising, broken blood vessels under the skin that look like tiny red spiders, loss of interest in sex and/or impotence, itching, swelling of legs and abdomen.

11. *Skin cancer*
    Symptoms: Sores that don't heal, lumps or growths that are firm to the touch and that grow or bleed, moles that are black or brown, have a splotchy appearance or an uneven border; moles that change size or shape; moles that itch or become sensitive.

God willing, you'll never have any of the diseases listed above. But a cold? Guaranteed. Unless you follow directions.

HOW TO PREVENT THE COMMON COLD

There's no cure yet, but while you're waiting try a few of these relief techniques:

- *Take lots of vitamin C.*
- *Take beta carotene:* 50,000–100,000 units a day in divided doses.

- *Cut out booze and coffee during cold season.*
- *Eat lighter and eat less* during cold season. If you eat a lot, your body has to work harder to digest the grub. But that same energy you're using to digest could be used to fight off any hideous cold cooties that try to invade the temple of your manhood.
- *Chop up two to four cloves of raw garlic* and swallow them with water. And stand over there, please.
- *Go to France.* The leading cold and flu medicine in Europe is Oscillococcinum, It stimulates the body's defense mechanisms and helps you fight off bugs.
- *Herbal medicines* like echinacea, goldenseal, and yarrow will help you fight off a cold.
- *Go classical:* Ancient Romans used to soak an onion in water, then sip the broth. Of course, they're all dead.
- *Go Revolutionary:* Similarly, eighteenth-century Americans drank a tea made of sage, hyssop, yarrow, black cohosh, buckthorn, goldenseal, coltsfoot, and bloodrot. A revolting brew, by the way.
- *Visit the juiceman* and drink lots of celery and grapefruit juice. Carrot juice. Carrot, celery, and parsley juice. Carrot and cucumber or carrot and beet, or mix all three.

Treatment

- *Drink a tea* of onion and garlic.
- *Breathe a steam* of water from a pot containing water with oil (or leaves) of eucalyptus, pine, cloves, or thyme.
- *Do a blue-bath healing:* You need a blue candle and some blue healing bath salts. Fill your tub with water and add a couple, three tablespoons of salts. Put one foot into the tub and feel the sickness drain from your body into the water. Repeat with other foot. Sit in the tub and feel the illness drain from your entire body. When the water becomes cool, drain the tub—don't get out—and watch your illness go down the drain. Use the shower to wash the remainder of the illness from your body.
- *New tea:* Garlic, green onion, basil, ginger, and mustard or cinnamon—boil for five minutes.

- *Take a fever bath* using marigold, thyme, lavender buds, pennyroyal, elder flowers, mugwort. Mix a quarter cup of each and soak it all in a quart of water. Once the mix is saturated, boil, then let it simmer for twenty minutes. Pour the liquid off into a bowl and pour that into a hot bath. Wrap the solids in a towel and rub over body while lying in tub.
- *Pray.*

ACHES, PAINS, AND OTHER COMPLAINTS

A small but eccentric collection of gripes:

How to Gracefully Wend Your Way down the Aisle

After a two-hour movie? Make sure you've spent your time with your feet flat on the floor, or, if that's too tight, with your ankles crossed. Either of these positions will relax the pressure on your legs. The worst position? One ankle over the thigh. It looks damned manly—and gives a nice presentation to those tube socks—but you're also temporarily shortening the leg muscle, curving your spine, and pinching the nerves in your leg. The result? Shooting pains from your heinie down to your toes.

How to Ride in Style

Walkin' like a cowpoke but ridin' a bike? Could be those sores are caused by a poorly adjusted saddle. Your bike's seat should be level and at a height where your knee is just slightly bent at the bottom of your pedal stroke. Also, trade those Lycra shorts in on some good, old-fashioned, 100 percent cotton briefs. Cotton absorbs moisture and makes for a more comfortable ride.

If your discomfort is coming at the other end of your body, take a look at your helmet. It should fit straight around your noggin and the straps should make a nice V just below your ears. Finally, shake your head. If the helmet shakes more than your head, adjust it.

How to Prevent Kidney Stones

Pass the stones, please. Life just too sissified for you, Arnold? Need a mansized pain challenge? Looking for a way to recapture the moral edge after your wife's gone through childbirth? Then forget rock climbing, say no to hang gliding, and skip the bungee. Go straight to *kidney stones!* What better way to show your woman you're a man than to pass some of those glasslike slivers right out the old willie?

The good news is you only have to show her once. After that, prevention is your likely choice. Here's what to know before you go:

- *Keep your piss watered down.* Drink water. Lots of it, too. Eight glasses a day. Give your whole body cavity a nice hydroponic environment. What's good for tomatoes is good for kidneys.
- *Add calcium.* The lab boys at Harvard studied 45,000 men—a stadiumful—and found those who consumed the most calcium had the *lowest* risk of peter-rocks.
- *Bogart that beef.* Vegetarians have only half as many stones as the rest of us. However, they have twice as much self-righteousness.
- *No salt.* That sodium crystal on your eggs is tomorrow's weenie-Gibraltar.

- *Up to your potassium in 'taters.* The same Harvard study that made the paradoxical calcium finding also discovered that high levels of potassium lower the risk of stones. Good sources: oranges, nectarines, spuds, and, of course, *bananas.*

How to Have a Date with a Coma

The planet's all-time favorite complaint? *I'm tired!* Fatigue following a good night's sleep can be a symptom of anything from obesity to depression to alcoholism. But not being able to fall asleep—well, that's an Everyman kind of problem.

Four golden solutions:

1. *Don't toss and turn* for more than twenty minutes. Get up and do something useful, but nothing strenuous.
2. *Hide the clock* and turn on some white noise. A small room heater turned to the "Fan Only" setting will even out extraneous noise.

3. *Exercise early* in the day. Revving up your body just before you park it doesn't do much to help induce a temporary coma.
4. *Use a relaxation technique.* Some guys count, some guys have sex, some guys pray. Some guys pray for sex—but that's no way to get sleep. Or sex. Or religion.

How Long to Pack a Twisted Ankle in Ice

First comes the icy walk, then comes the twisted ankle, then comes even more ice. But how much ice? And for how long? The answers: lots. For the second question, exactly twenty-five minutes, no more, no less. Researchers in Chicago found that if you take a gallon-sized plastic bag, fill it with ice, wrap it around the joint completely, and tape it in place, healing will start within five minutes and peak at twenty-five. After that: trouble. Icing for longer than a half hour can cause damage to the tissue and the nerves.

How to Give a Warm Round of Applause

To quickly warm up cold hands, swing your arms downward behind your body, then upward in front of you, like a crazed softball pitcher. Do it fast: About eighty swings per minute is what you want. The exercise drives blood to the fingers by using both gravity and centrifugal force.

How to Improve Everything

It's a **Main Thing** if ever there was a **Main Thing**: *Stop smoking.*

How to Add Three Inches to Your Height

Research suggests that *your posture is one of the first three things people notice about you.* Slouch and your world slouches with you, because, according to experts, you're sending a signal that you feel badly about yourself. Stand straight up for yourself, however, and you signal self-confidence. You also increase your energy by making it easier for your lungs to expand, help strengthen your abs and lower back muscles, and add up to three inches to your height.

How to Test for a Ruptured Achilles Tendon

Touch-football vets know how easy it is to rupture an Achilles tendon. The only good news is that it's even easier to test for one. This rupture test is almost always accurate—and you can do it at home. Here's how:

1. *Sit in a chair* with another chair in front of you. Extend your leg so your ankle is suspended over the edge of the second chair. Completely relax your leg.
2. *Squeeze the back of your leg* firmly just below the widest part of your calf muscle. If your tendon's in working order, your foot will automatically extend forward. If it doesn't, you may have a tear.

How to Dress Better for a Hernia

No truss, no muss. Say so long to that good-looking chunk of elasto-girdle you've been using to hold back the hernia time forgot. Doctors are using a mesh plug in place of old-fashioned in-patient hernial repair techniques. The advantages: lower cost, less cutting, less pain, less chance of recurrence, less time in the hospital. Disadvantages: less truss.

How to Groom the Beast

Covered with hair and worry, it's easy to forget how nice monkeys have it: Imagine, living in trees with whole tribes of cosmetologists, just picking and grooming.

Let's take this small subject from the top, starting with the all-time classic of instructional lit:

HOW TO USE SHAMPOO

Directions:
1. Lather.
2. Rinse.
3. Repeat.

Unfortunately, there's more to it than that. You have to know your hair.

- *Dry hair* is dry the entire length of the shaft to the scalp, which may itch and develop flakes. It seems like it never needs to be shampooed, and the ends look split, unkempt, and uneven. The texture of the hair is coarse. Often, gray or very curly hair is dry. Use a gentle shampoo every other day or so. Use an extra-rich conditioner.

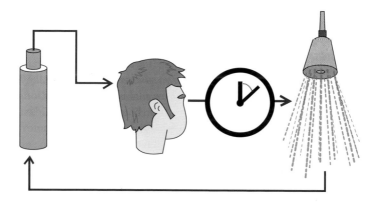

- ***Normal hair*** is smooth, usually free from breakage, and feels as if it has its own natural oil or source of moisture near the scalp. Shampoo when you like, using whatever you like.
- ***Oily hair*** has a tendency to feel damp. It has a shiny, silky texture, and by the end of the day, it's sticking to your scalp like a bad rug. It has to be washed every day. Unfortunately, frequent washing makes the problem worse, since the scalp will produce more oil to counteract the dryness resulting from the shampoo.

HOW TO TELL IF YOU'RE GOING BALD

Sorry you asked. If your hair has just begun thinning noticeably, you've already lost half of what you once had.

Digits from dandruff:
- Normal hair loss is 10–50 hairs per day.
- Slightly abnormal hair loss is 50–100 per day.
- Definitely abnormal hair loss is 100–150 per day.
- Almost toupee time: 150 or more per day.
  How soon? Depends:
- On the average blond head: 120,000 hairs.
- On the average brunette: 100,000 hairs.
- On the average redhead: 80,000 hairs.

Other ugly signs:
- Acne, now or ever.
- A flaky scalp (seborrhea).
- Development of bald patches (called alopecia areata).
- An increase in body hair or the appearance of body hair in unusual places.

Nine reasons guys go bald:
1. Poor scalp hygiene.
2. Low levels of estrogen.
3. Overuse of the wrong shampoos.
4. Too much dieting or rapid loss of weight.
5. High vitamin intake—vitamin A, in particular.
6. Too much brushing too hard.
7. Poor blood circulation—to the scalp especially.
8. Genetics.
9. Karma

- ***One more reason:*** So they'll never have to be middle-aged with their hair in a ponytail. However, *if you have a ponytail,* bald guys don't want you in their ranks. So use a coated rubber band to hold your hair instead of a clip. Clips will break and crease your hair.

HOW TO SHAVE

How to Brush on Lather

You have to have a badger-fur shaving brush. If you don't have it, you have to go out, find a badger, and negotiate. Once you run this luxurious fur across your face in the morning, you'll know you're never going back to a shaving creme can or gel.

The bulb of the brush fits into your hand like the joystick of an F-16. Stroke the bristles across your shaving soap, and then paint the lather across your face with to-and-fro strokes, letting the soft, water-soaked bristles of the brush massage open the pores of your skin for a much much better shave. You'll find badger-fur shaving brushes at a good department store, barbershop, or an old-fashioned neighborhood pharmacy. Expect to pay at least fifty bucks.

Face Facts

- The average male face has between 10,000 and 30,000 whiskers.
- Facial hair grows about fifteen-thousandths of an inch every day. That's as much as six inches a year.
- Over a lifetime, the average man will spend 125 days—3,000 hours—shaving.
- Collectively, men will spend $80 million this year on razors, $900 million on replacement blades.
- Thirty percent of that will be on electric shaving devices.
- Sixty percent of wet-shave razors sold are disposables.

How a Barber Gives a Shave

The widespread abandonment of America's barbershops by American men willing to pay one, two hundred dollars for a haircut to foreigners with one name is one of the red flags of growing national idiocy, and a reliable measurement of how deeply eroded common sense has become.

While barbers no longer get much respect, you have to remember that not too long ago, barbers did brain surgery, thus working both sides of the cranium. So just maybe we owe it to ourselves to reacquaint ourselves with these *nogginistes.* Also, barbershops are one of the few citadels of unsullied manhood left in this country: Big jars filled with blue Barbasol, the endless snip of scissors, the smell of shaving cream—in a barbershop, you've got everything a man needs, except women. Plus, you've got a normal guy there who will cut your hair pretty well. Maybe not great—but maybe your head of hair isn't all that great anyway.

Here's what you'll get from a barber—along with a healthy dose of your own self-respect back:

- ***First, he'll cover your face with hot lather.*** If you want to try this at home, throw your shaving cream into a sink full of hot water while you take a shower.
- ***Next, he covers your face—lather and all—with hot towels.*** This removes the fat and oils from your face.
- ***Then he relathers your face.*** Soap and a brush are more traditional, but the point of the lather is to get your skin and facial

hair follicles moist. Soap dries too quickly to keep the moisture contained. Today's creams and gels are more effective.

- *Then he starts to shave*—using a straight razor if he's any kind of barber at all.
- *On the first pass, he'll go with the grain.* Then he'll come back sideways. Going against the grain is a good way to donate blood. Going with the grain spares your skin, but spares your hairs at the same time. Thus, the second pass going sideways.
- *After the shave,* he applies menthol to your face and another hot towel.
- *To close your pores and prevent infection,* he'll give you a couple of slaps of astringent lotion.
- *A dash of talcum* finishes you off.

How to Give Yourself a Perfect Shave If You Can't Get to a Barber

Unless you're the Rockette of the watercooler, your face is about as much skin as company policy permits you to show around the office. Women? They've got those legs. But nobody makes pantyhose *specifically* for guys' faces, so it pays to take care of the mug you've got. How? By being careful how you use the mug you shave with. Here's how to scrape that winter beard off your face and make your skin smile at the prospect:

- *Get it clean.* Wash your face with warm water and mild soap. Use the occasion as an excuse to give yourself a kind of mug-massage by gently rubbing the soap into the skin. Rinse with warm water; you want to keep those pores wide open and happy.
- *Set it up.* The warm water will also keep your beard soft. Add a thick cream or a gel to lubricate your skin.
- *Cut it off.* In your ruthless ambition to cut every follicle's son, you'll want to shave against the grain. You'll be wrong. To avoid irritating your skin, shave with the direction of hair growth.
- *Thanks. You Needed That.* Think of shaving as petty surgery; the recuperation is as important as the way you wield the blade. So get tough: After you rinse the cream residue away, slap yourself around a little. Rubbing your skin dry is bad; patting your skin dry is good.

- *Use a weather sealant.* Not a deck finish, exactly, but maybe something that will both moisturize your skin and give it a little sunscreen at the same time.

How to Get Skinny

- **The Main Thing.** For those of us still toting some body fat, remember this:
3,500 CALORIES = ONE POUND OF FLESH.

  In other words, if you need to gain a pound by tomorrow, grease down a half-dozen Whoppers today, and you're there. Unfortunately, it doesn't work the other way around: To lose a pound by tomorrow, you have to work really hard today.

- *Here's why.* The average guy needs a couple thousand calories every day just to make the plant run: Your body's life-support system needs fuel to make the lungs breathe and the heart pump. So to lose a pound by tomorrow, not only do you have to eat nothing, you also have to burn up an additional 1,500 calories. So starve and spend the day on a marathon jog.

  Sensible men simply eliminate a burger or a brew and reduce their calorie intake by maybe 500 calories a day. At that rate, you'll lose a pound a week. Stay on this diet long enough and you'll cease to exist.

- *No deal!* It doesn't work that way, unfortunately. It's Zeno's dietary paradox: The more you lose, the harder you have to work to lose it. You cut back on the calories and your brain thinks you're losing weight and that that's good. But your body, the brainless idiot, thinks, "Starvation!" So it slows down your metabolic rate to make sure the rations you're supplying will be enough to go around.

- *Here's the diet cycle.* You diet. Your body slows down to counter the effect of the diet. You get frustrated because dieting doesn't work and so you go back to your old chow-hound ways and what happens? Your metabolism rate decreases to a rate that is even slower than what it was before you started dieting so what you ate before now causes you to add even more weight.

And that's why, if you want to lose weight, you need to exercise as well as reduce calories. The more you exercise, the higher your body's metabolic rate.

- ***It's common sense all the way.*** The federal government has a whole bunch of bureaucracies set up to tell you that the right way to get along with food looks like this:

  Eat a variety of foods.

  Maintain a healthy weight.

  Choose a diet low in fat, saturated fat, and cholesterol.

  Choose a diet with plenty of vegetables, fruits, and grain products.

  Use sugars only in moderation.

  Use salt and sodium only in moderation.

That's why every diet that works is a duh diet. Face it. If you live on beer and bread and weenies, you'll get fat. If you live on tofu and kelp, you'll get pompous and self righteous. But not plump.

HOW TO READ NUTRITION FACTS

Fat

You look like Oscar Mayer, but you want a body by Louis Rich. Between 3 and 5 percent of the fat in your body is called essential fat. It's the stuff in your nerves, spinal cord, and other organs. Think about this: Even your brain needs fat. Plus, it's what you might call the bare bones of padding, Nature's own version of packing peanuts. Alas, most guys' bodies are made up of something between 7 and 25 percent body fat. Average: 15. More than 25 is obese.

Fat watch. Looking at your percentage of body fat will tell you a lot more about your health than looking at your weight.

Sugar

Sugar is the Elvis of nutrients. It's *everywhere.* Look for terms such as "sucrose," "fructose," "maltose," "lactose," "honey," "syrup," "corn syrup," "high-fructose corn syrup," "molasses," or "fruit juice concentrate" in

the ingredient list. If one of these terms appears first, or if several are listed, the food is likely to be high in added sugars.

Naked calories. If you want to see what calories look like naked, take a gander at a whiskey sour. Alcohol and sugar—a miracle food. What better way to get fat and stupid at the same time?

- *From a breathalyzer's point of view,* a drink is the standard measurement of liquid idiot. Here's what's equal to one drink:
- A twelve-ounce can of beer.
- A glass of wine.
- A shot—one and a half ounces—of liquor.
- *Lite beers have fewer calories than regular beer,* but they'll get you just as drunk just as quick. Wine coolers and so-called light wines have less alcohol and fewer calories than regular wine.

Fiber

There'll come a time in your life, my dear chaps, when being regular will mean more to you than sex. The marketing department calls this "a Grape Nuts experience." But you know what we call it. Whole-grain breads, oatmeal, popcorn, and brown rice are the Mussolinis of the colon.

- *Fake fiber.* Some "wheat" breads have the same dark coloring as whole-wheat breads. But they're fakes. Sometimes caramel is used to give the bread that right color of brown, but there's not enough fiber in a loaf of the stuff to weave a sitcom plot.
- *Fake fat fiber.* The newly approved phony fat used as a dietary supplement in junk food—potato chips and the like—is really a

kind of fat-as-fiber, since it can't be broken down by your digestive system.

How to Grow a Huge, Disgusting Ball-shaped Belly

Eat a lot just before going to bed. Instant gut. If you eat most of your calories early in the day, you'll stimulate your body's ability to use energy, according to experts. Studies have shown that overweight people consume 75 percent or more of their calories in the evening, when their bodies are slowing down and are more likely to store fat. Eating large late is also a primary cause of potbellies, even among otherwise trim guys.

How to Eat Your Way Past a Bad Biopsy

The top-ten cancer-fighting foods, according to doctors and dieticians:

1. *Broccoli*
2. *Tomatoes*
3. *Spinach*
4. *Oranges*
5. *Garlic*
6. *Apples*
7. *Soybeans*
8. *Carrots*
9. *Hot red peppers*
10. *Green tea*

Other Stuff to Do to Get Fit

There are other things men do for exercise. For instance, they play golf. To some men, golf is an end in itself. To others, it's a means to a greater good.

HOW TO GET EXERCISE ON A GOLF COURSE

First, join a country club. Then rent a set of clubs and rent a cart. Drive out onto the course. Stop at the first tee. Grab a club—make it a two-iron—at both ends and rest it across the back of your shoulders for balance. Next, take a seat on the very front of the cart. Put your feet flat on the ground so your knees form a ninety-degree angle. Now slowly stand up until your back is straight, hold that position for a second, then *slowly* squat back down until your butt is just barely touching the cart. Hold that position for a second, then do it all over again. Do two sets of ten. Then climb back into the cart and drive straight back to the clubhouse.

Why it pays to rent golf gear if you're using the course as an outdoor gym: According to the National Sporting Goods Association, the cost of outfitting a golfer tip to toe with great golf stuff: more than $2,800. Almost three grand! Fore! What?

HOW TO PLAY FIVE DIFFERENT ONE-ON-ONE HOOP GAMES

Basic one-on-one is a game best suited to the office. Think about it: Those feints, dodges, and awesome full-extension Nerf power-dunks over the extended fingers of Griffin from the executive suite are downright dazzling— and all the more so because you're playing with a basket duct-taped to the wall above the copier. But transport the action to the gym or the playground, and one-on-one gets old fast. It inevitably deteriorates into a dispirited sequence of mindless posting up, thirty-foot prayers, and anemic sky hooks. The trouble is no one ever posts up in a real game, unless you're Charles Barkley and you've got a big butt.

When standard one-on-one leaves you uninspired, you need to find a new game. A game that challenges you and hones your skills at the same time. Funny you should ask. Our correspondent canvassed top NCAA basketball coaches around the country for their best ideas. Here's what they had to offer.

1. One-on-One, No Post

The rules: Simple. Standard one-on-one, but with a catch—no posting up. In other words, no turning your back on either your opponent or the basket. If you do, you immediately forfeit the ball. The only way to score is to drive straight for the basket or jump up and take your shot. First to 10 wins.

2. Beat the Clock

The rules: You stand beneath the basket with the ball. Your pal sprawls out on the sideline with a stopwatch. The minute-long drill begins after you knock down a quick layup. Then you're allowed only two dribbles in any direction before you have to square up to the basket, shoot, and hustle for the rebound. Once you grab the ball, repeat the same steps: two dribbles, shoot, rebound. Swish as many as you can until your partner calls time. Then you take the watch and he's up. Each basket scores one point, and the winner is whoever scores the most in five one-minute bursts.

3. Rhythm Method

The rules: You camp out anywhere along the three-point arc, while your opponent stands under the basket with the ball. He passes it to you and immediately pops out to stick a hand in your face while you shoot the jumper. If you make it, he quickly retrieves the ball and repeats the process as you launch different shots from about eighteen feet. If you miss, you grab the rebound, and now it's his turn to go to the perimeter. The game flows back and forth without missing a beat until someone scores ten points. Each bucket earns one point.

4. Around-the-World Adjustable

The rules: Let's say you want to play your eight-year-old son, who stands just four feet, nine inches. Here's how to equalize the situation. Select five ten-foot shots for him and five corresponding twenty-foot shots for yourself. Then apply standard around-the-world rules: With each basket you make, you advance to the next position. If you miss the basket, you have two options: either give up the ball or take an extra turn. If you do elect to try again and miss, you go back to the starting position. The winner is the first player to hit his five shots going around and coming back.

5. Rough House

The rules: If you're feeling a bit sinister, you might try this aggression-testing favorite. One player must dribble in from a dead-ball stop at mid-court against a minimum of four opponents. Everyone defends as he attempts to score. Once he shoots, getting the rebound is a free-for-all. Whoever grabs it resets at midcourt, and the cycle repeats. It's every man for himself, and the first to hit seven baskets wins.

TWO PICK-UP BASEBALL GAMES REQUIRING SIX PEOPLE OR LESS

1. Hit the Bat

One guy's up, everybody else isn't. Guy at bat hits the ball—even a softball will do—to the field, then lays the bat down on the ground. The player catching the ball then tries to roll or toss the ball so that it hits the bat. The batter must then catch the ball as it ricochets up and off the bat. If he doesn't, the player who hit the bat is up.

2. Three Flies

One guy's up, everybody else isn't. The guy at bat hits flies to the field. Whoever catches three flies is up next. Note: The batter must hit fly balls. Grounders count as strikes. If the batter strikes out, the last person to shag a fly is up.

HOW TO CATCH THE LAST FOUL BALL OF THE SEASON

Want proof that God invented baseball? Science guys say the universe was the size of a Spalding regulation hardball just before the big bang. This same miracle of theoretical physics is replicated hundreds, thousands of times every season. Sometimes, these nascent universes curve up and away and land in the stands, where they become objects of veneration. How to best improve your odds of walking away with a souvenir of God's love for mankind?

- ***Know your pitchers:*** A fastball pitcher will generate a lot more foul balls than a guy who throws curves and other off-speed stuff.

- *Sit tight, sit right:* Hitters swing late at fastballs, so they'll either foul a pitch straight back behind the plate or they'll pop one into the opposite field stands—the first-base side for a right-handed batter, third for a lefty. *So you have two options:* Either sit in the first level behind home plate—a little to the right for a left-handed batter, or a little to the left of the plate for a righty—in order to snag a rising foul ball. Or you can sit back in the lower deck at about a thirty-degree angle from the first- or third-base bag.

- *For batters who get ahead of the pitch:* Snag those bullets from seats back along a line equidistant between the outfield wall and first or third base.

- *The best ballparks for foul shaggers:* Atlanta, Anaheim, and Detroit for balls fouled back of home plate. For shots hit foul down the lines, try Philly, St. Louis, Houston, Yankee Stadium, and, of course, Fenway Park in Boston and Chicago's Wrigley Field.

- *If all else fails:* Head south this winter. Winter leagues offer sparse crowds, small ballparks, and slow-moving competition from other foul hunters in the stands.

4. Work and Intelligence

Lucky women. They are what they are. But men? We're nothing more than what we do. And how smart we are.

Why do we hate working hard to get smart? Well, there are two things wrong with smart. First off, it hurts your head. Heads are products of their times, and these aren't the brightest of days. You think too much with a modern head, and you can blow the sucker right up. A hundred years ago, when kids had to know Latin just to get into high school, heads were made of cast iron. Today, we get a polyresin job, and that's if we're lucky. Lots of guys just get mush with a plate on it.

Second off, smart doesn't just happen to you. For example, you can't just go to the beach, look at butts, eat sno-cones, and come back home smarter than when you left. To get smart, you have to get out there and catch it, make it happen, and stick it behind your eyes so you can find it later, in case you need it.

How to Lift Heavy Thoughts Without Hurting Yourself

Work your way into it, bit by bit, starting with the basics.

STUFF TO THINK ABOUT

Most of us could use a good thought now and then. For instance, here's a list of all the things every man ought to know:

- How to run a chain saw.
- When to buy a stock index option.
- The difference between a brook and a brown trout.
- The current value of his 401(k).
- The meaning of life.
- How to start an outboard.
- The difference between a beef and a dairy cow on sight.
- How to change the oil.
- What a woman wants.
- What time the game starts.

From this small list we can see there's a difference between industrial strength cogitating and simple common knowledge. It's not as if you have to think your way through an oil change. If you don't know *exactly* how to change the oil, the guy next door does, and he'll tell you. In fact, all this stuff is the substance of comfortable masculine chat, the conversational topics that have instant and undeniable appeal because they are things that we know we ought to know, even if we don't. All of them, that is, except that "meaning of life" thing, which is something we talk about with others guys about as often as we swap tales of religious conviction or really helpful masturbatory techniques. "What's the meaning of life?" is one of those questions that's so big and so important, the only time it ever comes up is when it's the punchline of a joke.

TIME TO GET MENTALLY FIT

Certainly, we all know that our mission as postmodern men is to fight flab wherever we find it. We know that the longer we put off a workout the harder it becomes, and that you can only ignore the obvious symptoms of laziness for so long. Fitness is fitness, so maybe what we need is a way to hone our philosophical fitness, really work the stiffness out of our ethical joints and moral muscles. The object of the game ought to be to come up with a personal philosophy of some kind, a Nautilus for the noggin. It ought to be something a guy can really use, a contraption perched on a solid base, with lots of room for weighty considerations, and all held together by some durable, highly polished principles. It ought to be the kind of thing which, if constructed carefully, can help a chap stay in shape for a lifetime. Your head is where you put the thing together, and where you use it until your brain hurts.

And then what good is it? Well, use it or lose it.

THREE FOOLPROOF WAYS YOU CAN START THINKING OLYMPIC-SIZED THOUGHTS FAST

1. ***Avoid light thinking.*** Modern thought is like modern water. There's a lot of it around, but most of it's unsuitable for human consumption. Besides, most of what resembles thought is really the kind of stuff you'd like to keep out of a place devoted to do-it-yourself philosophizing. Philosophies are built on large,

complex thoughts, the kind of thing you will never see, for example, on the tail end of a car, where people are most likely to confuse what they feel with what they think. "Another Mother for Peace" has one 100 percent of the minimum daily adult requirement for feel-good sentiment. It also contains almost no useful thought, which, as you know, is the fiber of a good philosophy.

2. *Work out in silence.* Our culture is chock full of talking devices. Everybody wants to talk; everybody wants to be heard, whether or not they have anything to say. A century ago, formal discourse was considered an art practiced by the likes of Oscar Wilde and George Bernard Shaw, and good conversation came dear. Now we get Barbara Walters and Pat Buchanan, and talk is cheap, mostly because there's so much of it around. Because talking is not the same as thinking, there are two obvious things to keep out of a good home think-gym: a TV set and a phone. One thing to install: a decent bookshelf. Before you accept anybody's idle chatter as a bona fide idea, do what any sensible man would do: get it in writing.

3. *Increase resistance gradually but consistently.* Of course, a stick-built philosophy is only worth whatever you put into it. Since, as a rule, philosophies are designed to answer tough questions, it helps to know which ones to ask. Happily, life is supply-side crazy when it comes to providing thoughtful questions with built-in gradations of difficulty. Forget the big, huge philosophical questions like "What is love?" and "What is beauty?" Instead, start with some smaller, entry-level questions that are kind of open-ended. For example, "What am I doing here?"—the self-directed variant on "Hey! What're you doing here?"—is a superb question, one in which the difficulty of the answer can be ratcheted up in infinitely small increments, like a conceptual Soloflex. It's a take-anywhere question you can ask yourself any time in any circumstance, and it will always have an immediate effect: It'll help you define yourself, and it'll help you get philosophically fit fast. It might also save you a lot of trouble. For example, at lunch, Cheryl, the Madonna of marketing, notices a tiny speck of ratatouille on your cheek, and reaches over, pressing her perfect breasts hard against

you, and carefully, *seductively*, wipes it away with one hand, while resting her other hand high on your thigh, dreadfully close to the lap devil, the blind idiot, the muscle that knows no morality. Just as you catch her hand in yours, you ask, "What am I doing here?" and bingo! the dogs of divorce are banished into the night. Asking the same question when you're alone in your home think-o-drome can also bring unexpected results.

- *Caution:* Beginners beware. If you experience pain or discomfort, lighten up. Do what I do: Stretch a little by asking yourself a slightly smaller question, like, "Wonder what's for dinner."

Pretty soon you'll be ready for an iron-man thinkathon. Read on.

How to Get Brain Buff

Wise up! According to experts, the world's a dumber place than ever. The evidence of growing stupidity is everywhere. Test scores are tumbling. Blissful ignorance is on the rise. Schoolkids can't read or write. If stupid hurt, the whole planet would be a world of pain.

Hello and good-bye to the Knuchlehead Nineties. But wait! If you think about it, it's also a time of unparalleled opportunity. There's a bundle to be made outsmarting other guys—plus, women really like men with a little headmeat to go with those perfect abs.

So get to know your noggin. Be smart! And if you can't do that, at least *look* smart! Buy glasses! Wear tweed! Memorize tapes! Figure out how much you really need to know, *minimum*. Like the magazines say, get fit fast! But get smarter faster!

By the way, our trusty correspondents here are the guys at *Men's Health*, and especially our friend Dave. The *Men's Health* chaps are simply *rolling* in info. They probably had seven, eight million useful tips on how to get real smart lickety-split. But they only gave us fifty or so. They're not *stupid,* you know.

HOW TO THINK FAST

Concepts! Incoming!

Keep on Running

Senator Strom Thurmond is ninety-three, and a member of the Senate Judiciary Committee, which means he's smart enough to sit around and talk about Clarence Thomas's sex life with guys like Joe Biden and Ted Kennedy. Want smarter? Here's smart with a spritz of stamina: Thurmond has been running for the Senate every six years since 1954, and he's won every race. That's brain endurance all the way. How does he do it? Exercise, of course. He says:

- *To keep your brain working well, you have to exercise* to keep the arteries that take blood to the brain clear for nutrients, and to help push the blood there with your muscles. I swim a half mile twice a week and I do ten minutes of stretching, twenty minutes of calisthenics, and twenty minutes of stationary cycling every morning. If you can do all that, there aren't many things you won't be able to do.

- *Other smart guys agree.* One study in California found that people who exercise routinely actually think better, remember more, and react more quickly than people who don't exercise at all. And an Illinois study found that subjects who exercised scored 30 percent higher on auditory and visual tests than sedentary subjects.

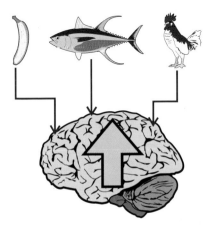

Feed Your Head

Your brain is as selective as the bouncer at a chic New York nightclub. When you eat, your body devours the protein, carbohydrates, fats, vitamins, and minerals in the chow, then converts them into membranes and chemicals your brain will use to learn, think, feel, and remember. However, if one particular amino acid isn't up front and noticed, chances are that nutrient will be ignored and left standing at the door. And just like the nightclub scene, who gains entrance sets the mood for the rest of the night. Here's what you need to get in:

- **Bees.** The buzz in brain functioning comes from the B vitamins—especially B6—found in oats, tuna, chicken, whole wheat, and bananas. Smart researchers in Holland figured this out by giving a bunch of healthy seventy-year-old guys twenty milligrams of B6 every day for twelve weeks. They found that the B6 men did better on tests of long-term memory than a control group who had been given a placebo. Other B vitamins (specifically numbers 1, 2, 3, and 12) boost mental energy, too. Check with your pharmacist.
- **Hold back on carbohydrates.** Carbohydrates are what you need to eat if you're a guy who wants to lift heavy objects. Carbohydrates are what you need to avoid, however, if you want to be the guy smart enough to decide which heavy objects the carbo eaters ought to lift. A meal that's loaded with carbohydrates equals trouble for the brain.

   Here's the science: Carbohydrates contain the amino acid *tryptophan,* which competes with another crucial amino acid, *tyrosine,* to enter the brain, and you need tyrosine to be a smart guy.
- **Tyrosine** is crucial to quick thinking, fast reactions, and feelings of alertness, which pretty much describes how smart guys feel most of the time, especially when they're talking to beautiful tyrosine women who can use their tongues to pronounce foreign words, such as *zeitgeist* and *cul-de-sac.*
- **Tryptophan** slows reaction time, impairs concentration, makes you sleepy, and reduces the need to be in control. Tryptophan is the drug of choice for morons. Comes free with Whoppers.
- **How to stay smart all the way through lunch.** Eat the protein food *before* you eat the carbo food. And make sure that your ratio

of carbohydrates to protein isn't more than three to one. Four ounces of tuna and two slices of bread, or a chicken breast and baked potato will do the trick.

- ***Eat less, think more.*** Graze, don't feast. Feasting causes a drop in energy because it shunts blood to the digestive tract—instead of your brain. Try to eat several small, witty, clever meals a day, instead of three big, stupid ones.

HOW TO THINK CLEARLY

Watch the Clock

If you want to use your smarts, use them while they're hot. For most of us, that means midmorning meetings and early lunches. Every day, you wake up dumb, then get smarter and smarter until around noon. Then it's downhill to dumb again, which strikes most of us sometime in the late afternoon. Then you make a slight intellectual recovery. But around ten or so, you're on the slippery slope of idiocy again, until you slide into the nightly coma, the end of the ride.

Use Your Head

Might as well. It's there, sticking out of the top of your shirt, holding open your collar, making sense of your ears. You might as well use it. Besides, your brain is like the other use-it-or-lose-it organ. If you neglect it, it gets permanently soft. Smart guys solve crosswords, read theology, analyze DH choke stats, or talk to their wives about money just to give

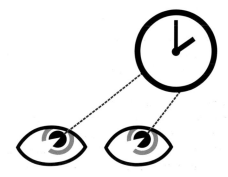

the old noodle a workout. Hard thinking causes neural circuits to flash into action. Suddenly, capillaries expand, neurotransmitters zip back and forth, and blood flow increases. The result? A brain that stays younger longer. And your ability to handle complex issues—things that involve both reasoning and remembering—will remain strong five or ten years longer than those who aren't mentally active.

- **_Hung like Einstein's dendrites:_** Curious researchers at UCLA's Brain Research Institute, examining the brains of twenty dead adults, found that gray matter from college grads who remained mentally challenged throughout life had up to 40 percent longer _dendrites_—the branchlike parts of nerve cells that bring in information and help promote sophisticated processing—than the brains of people who had less than a high-school education and whose idea of advanced problem solving was trying to figure out what to watch on TV. Dumb people had dendrites so short you could sink a fifty-yard putt in their brainpan. Longer dendrites mean a greater surface for synaptic connections. The longer your dendrites, the better your noggin. Also with longer dendrites, you get free! bonus! _glial cells,_ which nourish and support neurons and are known to increase in number with learning and experience. Smart guys can make their noggins into big, buff, lush, wet, glial plantations—with dendrites like wild capellini—by doing something they've never done before, brainwise, like learning Portuguese or figuring out what women want. The brain is a muscle. If you exercise it, it gets bigger and stronger. Like that other eyeless, one-track, brief-bound brain of yours. The number-one dendrite fertilizer? Hanging out with people smarter than you are.

And get this: In the early 1980s, UC Berkeley researchers, looking into the egghead of well-known thinkperson Albert Einstein, discovered the goofy-haired genius had longer dendrites in his brain than normal, less relativistic guys. In other words, _the inside of Einstein's head looked exactly like the outside!_

HOW TO REMEMBER WHAT YOU LEARN

Simply relaxing can significantly enhance your ability to learn something.

Be Blissfully Bright

In a Stanford study of thirty-nine people between the ages sixty-two and eighty-three, members of one group were taught to relax every muscle in their body from head to toe, whereas those in the other groups got a lecture about how to improve their attitude toward aging. The findings: ***The group that had practiced consciously relaxing their body before a three-hour memory-training course was able to remember 25 percent more*** than the groups that had not relaxed. Remember that.

Forget the Face

But remember the name. Sometimes when you meet people, you're so busy trying to impress them or struggling to keep the conversational rolling that the name breezes right by you and never enters your conscious mind. The key to remembering a name?

- ***Concentrate*** on the person you're meeting.
- ***Play around with the name*** for a moment or two in your mind.
- ***Say it*** at least once to yourself.

What you need is to rehearse the name in what scientists call a distributed fashion. To do this, repeat the name to yourself a few times, waiting an extra second each time you repeat it, until there are four or five seconds between sayings of the name. Example: You're introduced to your new boss, Jim Bozo. Say "Bozo, Bozo, Bozo" softly to yourself until you think you've got it.

Remember Important Events

Memories aren't always carbon copies of events. In fact, your mind is in a constant editing mode, changing the original memory so that it reflects newly acquired facts. Stuff that happens after an important event can significantly alter your recollection of the event.

To ensure you remember something exactly as it happened, to recall a business meeting or the negotiating terms of a major contract, write it down in detail *immediately afterward*. Then review it—aloud, if necessary. This records the memory while it's fresh, reinforces the memory by freezing it in place, and provides you with an opportunity to review what really happened so the original memory doesn't fade or get distorted.

Remember What You Read

Remember the last time you read a book? No, no. Not this one. The *last* one. Remember? Okay. Remember how, five minutes after you put it down, you couldn't remember anything in it? You've got a recall problem bigger than GM's biggest nightmare. Here are three ways to retain what you read:

1. ***Get the big picture.*** Use the table of contents to map the book and quickly find what you want to read. Skim through the index and look for things you already know a little something about, and flip to the parts of the book where they're discussed. Read the introduction or preface.

2. ***Skip it.*** Feel perfectly comfortable skipping the parts that don't really look interesting. Your interest is dictated by what you need to know. If it doesn't intrigue you, you don't need to learn it.

3. ***Reduce the book or article to about six key terms.*** Try to visualize the key players and events, and analyze the relationships between them. Ask yourself questions about what's in the article. In a novel, such as *Moll Flanders,* imagine yourself in the scene as one of the characters, dealing with the problems before him.

HOW TO LEARN TO DO TWO THINGS AT ONCE

Tune in: There is no Jerry Ford clinic. If there were, though, it would be devoted to helping guys do two things at once. One of the easiest ways to learn how to do so without dividing your attention is to put two TVs next to each other, tune them to different channels, and try to listen to both at once. See how much information you can absorb from each and try not to miss a thing. Once you're able to do this well, you can use the TVs to learn how to resist distractions. This time, instead of trying to take in everything from both TVs, concentrate on one program and ignore the other. It'll be hard at first, but stay with it. When you think you've mastered it, try lowering the volume on the set you're watching and raising it on the one you're not. If it doesn't drive you crazy first, this technique is guaranteed to teach you how to pay attention effectively.

- ***Downside:*** You have two TV sets going, and nothing worth watching on either one.

HOW TO SPD RD

Fourstepsforeadingfasterthanabullet:

1. ***Preview what you're going to read first.*** Look at the titles, sub-heads, pull-quotes, or anything that's in *italics* or **boldfaced.** The author wants you to pick up on facts, concepts, and other important information.

2. ***Use your hand as a pacer to underline what you're reading*** and keep you moving rapidly through the material. The primary bene fit? It's a concentration tool that keeps you focused on what you're reading. If you're focused, you'll retain more.

3. ***Read groups of words.*** Words are meant to trigger thoughts. Hea-ring everything in your head—as opposed to just seeing it—can actually slow your thinking. Start reading words in groups of twos and threes, and increase the number as your skill improves.

4. ***Read vertically.*** Left-to-right eye movement wastes a lot of time and causes you to read *everything,* most of which isn't all that important. If you keep your left-to-right eye movement at a mini-mum as you go down the page, your eye can take in swaths of up to 3,500 words a minute.

HOW TO BUILD A GOOD EDUCATION

If you want to prove yourself invaluable, try to become an expert on something. Keep it in the ballpark, though. If you're working in ship-ping, don't try to study microbiology at home in your spare time.

- ***A little expertise is a cool thing.*** People who excel—whether it's in sports, or business, or the professions—spend a lot of time studying, even if they don't like to admit it. So do your home-work. Spend a half hour going over some aspect of your job—or, if you're angling for a move, someone else's. It takes very little effort to get a leg up on other guys who don't take the time to increase their value.

- ***Home school.*** You can give yourself a tremendously wide liberal arts education by focusing on the one thing that interests you most—say, sex or canoeing—and slowly but tirelessly learning everything there is to know about the subject. The history of the world can be told in canoes or in fellatio. One thing leads to another, and if you programmatically follow each and every lead, pretty soon you'll know all there is to know.

No short cuts to smart. Once you get a good grasp, knowledge builds. What you already know helps you take the next step. At the foundation, the main areas must be history, English, math, and science. Once you understand them pretty well, everything builds on itself and comes together.

HOW TO IMPERSONATE A SMART PERSON

In the end, of course, there will always be limits to how smart anybody can be. If you feel like your cranium is running at redline and you just can't get any smarter, then punt. *Fake it.* Imitation smart, with the look and feel of the real thing, isn't the same as dumb, after all. Here's how to pretend:

How to Look Smart

Once you strip away professional considerations, it's much easier to look intelligent than you might think. According to a recent study conducted by a German university, people will think you're intelligent if:

- You are attractive.
- You are reasonably fit.
- You seem friendly and self-assured.
- You dress conservatively.
- You wear your hair in a stylish fashion.

You'll be perceived as less than smart if you "look unrefined," dress unstylishly or informally, or appear to be out of shape.

In addition, people with round faces look, to those surveyed, dumber than people with long or oval faces.

However, these factors all faded in significance once verbal expression was factored in. People who were ultimately rated highest in intelligence demonstrated high levels of verbal skills, which include

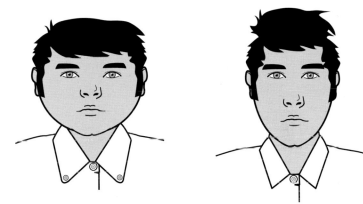

Figure 1. Dumb   Figure 2. Smart

- Clear articulation of ideas.
- A pleasant voice.
- A lack of halting or confused speech.

Psychologists no longer rely exclusively on the standard IQ test as a sole indicator of intelligence. Researchers have, until recently, not paid much attention to how people perceive intelligence in others.

HOW TO BE VAGUE

The smarter you are, the greater your ability to be specific and to articulate your thoughts with precision. *Really* smart people can operate at such a refined level of erudition that to mere mortals, they sound like Zen wind chimes. This is good for dumb but wily guys, since they know it means that if they can successfully mimic the inscrutability of a genuinely smart person, those around them may also assume that they're a genuinely smart guy, too.

For example, Employer X, in his own ethereal manner, would sometimes be overheard by others in the office saying to a subordinate, "When they zig, you zag," or, "I don't know what I don't know." If you're concerned with the appearance of smart and not the *reality* of smart, this is a good tactic. Tonally pleasing gibberish can also lubricate a guy out of a tight spot.

HOW TO BE ESOTERIC

Better than vague, more colorful than smart, esoteric really works at pushing a brainy persona. Why? Because since almost everybody graduating from college these days has a vocational training and not a fundamental education, it's pretty easy to enhance your smart-guy image by simply leap-frogging a lot of dead Greeks and other white, male Euro-types, and going straight for the obscure and arcane. If you read five books about, say, Tibetan Buddhism, you'll know more about the subject than almost anybody in America.

How to Be Tolerable

You can win lots of friends and influence lots of people in the time it takes to have a simple conversation:

- When someone is talking, **suspend your judgments** until that guy has had his say.
- *Lean forward slightly,* nod, make eye contact, and ask clarifying questions.
- *Don't take up all the airtime.* Even if it's your program, give the other guy a chance to ventilate.
- *Develop the art of mirroring.* This is almost totally craven, but it works like a charm. What you do is try to imitate in subtle ways the person you want, to like you. Human beings crave being with people who seem to be like themselves. This means if someone is talking to you and leaning forward at forty-five degrees, you do the same. If someone you're with crosses his legs, you do the same. If the other guy loosens his tie—well, you get the picture. To everybody else, you'll look like a couple of loose Rockettes. But to the person who matters, these small gestures will subconsciously make your acquaintance feel as if you're some kind of kindred soul, and, chances are, he'll like you for it.

How to Make Friends You Can Count On

Sometimes, friends die. Sometimes, friendships die. Either way, it's a painful deal. Ugly truth: Holding on to friends is tough. Uglier question: At any given moment, how many friends do you think you have? We're talking friends, here, not acquaintances, employees, or hangers-on, but honest-to-goodness, post-your-bail, ignore-your-buck-naked-wife friends. How many? Two? Four? One? Most men have a couple. Nobody ever has more than five genuine, true-blue friends at any one time.

What accounts for this lifelong shortfall of compadres, amigos? It's the difficulty of the rules. Friendship is a game so complex that only sheer luck allows you to bump into somebody else who plays the game just the way you'd do, who does unto you as you do unto, who behaves just the way you'd behave in a friendship. If you think your friends are people who can help you, or people who adore you, or people who will make you feel swell about yourself, you've got no friends at all. The recognition of your own values in somebody else is usually all it takes to put the good-pal seal of approval on an acquaintanceship. Most of these rules are vague and unwritten; they can only be intuited. But there are some things all friends can agree on:

MAINTENANCE IS OPTIONAL

One very nice thing about a friend is that you can take important aspects of his friendship for granted. This is important because most men's lives become more complex as they approach midlife. You spend your first thirty, forty years getting a life. Then all of a sudden, you have too much of one. As your responsibilities grow, your career and your family claim increasing amounts of time—and when you do get a free minute, it usually goes to some immediately accessible source of amusement, like golf-ball abuse or fish slaughter.

Here's the real-life priority list for most modern men:
1. Your family.
2. Your friends.
3. Your job.

For most men, it's a tight race between one and two, but generally it's three that demands the most attention. Still, this is the batting order, and if your priorities are different, you're in bad shape. However, real friends won't make you rock the boat with numbers one or three just to massage number two. For instance, friends don't need to see your face every day to know whether you're still a friend. Most men assume the quality of their friendship is sturdy, rustproof, and low-maintenance. Friends know their friends will be their friends until further notice, and that's really all they need to know.

TIME IS NOT OF THE ESSENCE

Lonely, friendless people claim that friendships must stand the test of time. They are incorrect. Friendships that must be tested by time (or by anything else, for that matter) generally fail the test. Your best pal may be somebody you've known for less time than it takes to run a pennant race, or it may be somebody your grandmother knew as a child.

FRIENDSHIPS ARE MUTUAL

For a friendship to flourish, there must be equal opportunity for friendship on both sides. If you have a chum who never asks for anything, ever, it's impossible to treat him like a friend. Then you have to decide if it's possible to be friends with somebody who won't let you be friendly.

DUTY CALLS

Here's where the vinyl siding peels off a friendship: Friends must be defended when they're wrong, explained when they're irrational, respected when they're defiled. Friendship carries with it certain unpleasant duties. Ideally, they are rarely, if ever, required. But when duty calls, you can't dodge the draft.

Note: Defending your friend when he's wrong is one thing. You also have a duty to tell your friend when he's wrong, even as you defend him. He also has a duty not to put you in ridiculous situations for the sake of a friendship.

ALL SUCCESSES ARE SHARED

Well, this is true up to a point. You don't have a right to expect your friend to exploit his hard-won success by giving you its benefits. But you're bound by the rules of friendship to be genuinely glad for your friend's successes. You can also be envious, of course. You can even consider the success ill-deserved. But when a friend hits a homer, you have to cheer, even if you're batting zip.

How to Improve Your Self-esteem

You're one helluva guy, even if you don't think so. Want proof? Okay:

HEY, YOU'VE GOT TO BE BETTER THAN SOMEBODY

Beijing bunters: In the summer of 1978, John Lowenstein, a left fielder for the Baltimore Orioles, came to bat in a late inning with the game on the line. He bunted. The ball floated high into the air, then lazily descended into the glove of the needlessly alert pitcher. There was a soft puff, then a thousand groans filled the night. Later, in the locker room, sportswriters surrounded Lowenstein wanting to know what had gone wrong, but, in the manner of good newsmen, afraid to tackle the subject head-on for fear of hurting an athlete's feelings. "That was a terrible bunt, John," one of them finally said. His colleagues murmured nervously.

"You know," said Lowenstein, apparently uninjured, "every time I bunt like that I think of China."

"China?" asked the writer. "How come China?"

"Because," said Lowenstein gravely, "there are a billion Chinese. And I'm a better bunter than all of them."

There's a corollary to this little law:

YOU'RE LUCKIER THAN YOU KNOW

Sure, not everything breaks for you. The schmuck in the next cubicle got his promotion the lucky way, while you actually had to work for yours. And it's quite true that if you had been in the right place at the right time your entire life would be completely different than it is today. But, in fact, it might be worse. True story: In 1982 in Yugoslavia, a farmer was walking along a road when suddenly a storm blew up: rain, thunder, and lightning, lots of lightning, a bolt of which hit our man and killed him. Bad luck, you say? There's more: This was, it turned out, the second time this guy had been struck by lightning. Plus, when he passed away, he joined his two brothers, his father, his aunt, two uncles, and his maternal grandfather in bad-break hell. Seriously. They had all been killed by lightning strikes.

You're luckier than dead people, and don't you forget it. At least you're alive! Feel the wind in your hair! Feel the rain on your face! Hear the thunder! See the lightning! Stand tall! Reach up to the heavens with that metal-tipped umbrella of yours! You're alive!

- **Now. Use what you've learned.** Compared to many men, you're a witty, accomplished, lucky Don Juan, laughing your way through a life that, by any reckoning, is better than a couple of other guys' lives. Still a nonbeliever? If this were an article in a women's magazine, we'd give you a little quiz to help reveal the phenomenal worth of the you you really are. But we're men here, healthy men, so no matter what you scored, you'd be on the brink of an esteem breakthrough. Think about it: You're a helluva guy. We love you, you love you, we're all as happy as can be. In fact, forget us. Let's talk about you. You're marvelous, you big lug, you. You're wonderful. But, hey, you already know that.

How to Find a Job

The best way to meet really charming and beautiful women is to get married. Ten minutes after your wedding ceremony, all the women you sought during your miserable bachelor sex-drought will be at your feet.

Same thing with jobs. When you don't need them, they're a dime a dozen. The best advice? Ease the pressure by turning up the income. Take a job, *any job.* Take a job at a beach resort as a lifeguard. Take a job as a car salesman. Take a job doing something you know is going nowhere. Wait until you get two or three checks under your belt. Then pursue your job search in a pleasant and leisurely fashion. Bosses are like women—often, bosses are women—and if they think you're desperate, the kind of man nobody wants, they're not going to want you either.

Four more ways to a regular payday:

1. **Don't whine.** Tell anybody who asks that you *like* the job you have. Even if the guy who asks is the personnel director at Acme Incorporated, and even if the job you have is busing tables at IHOP. But, of course, you can add that you'd obviously like to be doing something more interesting.

2. **Don't shortchange yourself.** Trading time and effort for money is as basic a barter as any man makes, and if you're going to be successful in any kind of horse trade, you have to know what your horse is worth. If you can't be realistic about your marketable skills, ask a friend to help you set a fair price.

3. **See the moves.** If you have to choose between a good job in an industry in which you have no interest, and a lousy job in an industry you find fascinating, take the lousy job. In other words, when you look around for a job, deal with the industry as a whole. You may have to take a job in the mail room, but if you're smart and good and work hard, it's not the job you'll have in five, seven, ten years. You have to see the whole road. If you don't know where you're going, you'll never get anyplace.

4. **Hide your ambivalence.** Every job has a downside, but no job has a downside as big as the downside to having no job at all. Opportunity is sometimes a moving target; don't hesitate to take your best shot.

HOW TO DECIDE ON A JOB

Of all the questions asked by suffering correspondents looking for cheap advice about jobs, the question "What should I do next?" is asked more often than any other one.

Well, here's the answer no job-searching man wants, but at least it's the truth: ***It doesn't matter.***

JACK RABBIT
X-ING

A personal observation—and a big **Main Thing:** *Any time you have to make a decision, remember that any decision is better than none. Here's how I came by this cheap insight: My friend Denis Boyles was riding with his grandfather, Claude Boyles, in his huge, old Chrysler just outside nowhere, Kansas, when a jackrabbit jumped out in the middle of the road.* "Now, watch," *he said. The car kept a constant speed. The rabbit feinted left, feinted right, then left again, then right, then, at the last minute, just as the car was right on top of him, left again, and right under the tires, flat. Denis was upset.* Claude Boyles said, "The problem was he couldn't make up his mind. It wouldn't have mattered either way."

A good lesson; animals have died for less. The problem with not making a decision is that if you don't, events—those big Chryslers on the thoroughfare of woe—will make the decision for you. People spend years responding to crises and reacting to events, and feel miserable because they have no control over their lives. Can't decide between Acme and Consolidated or between the army and college? No problem. Flip a coin: Heads, you join the army. Tails, you go back to college. It really doesn't matter, because everything else will work itself out. The only thing that matters is that you choose.

HOW TO SPOT A JOB TO AVOID

Here's another **Main Thing:** *Never take a managerial job in a family business if you aren't a member of the family.* You'll be cheated and mistreated, pushed from one side of the family to the other, and you'll never be loved. Instead, you'll be fired.

HOW TO TALK ABOUT WORK

The most important conversations about work are the ones you have with the chap driving the personnel desk. That first interview is the make-or-break chat, the one that says, "You're hired!"—unless you say otherwise. According to the president of a Dallas recruitment firm, here are the three deadliest mistakes an interviewee makes:

1. *Not listening.* Don't jump into the interviewer's question. Let him ask the question, make the comment, declare the obvious without help from you. The interviewer doesn't care what your agenda is. He wants to know that you understand *his.*

2. *Holding back.* Show a little interest when the interviewer tells you about the nuances of Eastern European tractor production. One tip: Lean forward when you speak to create a sense of involvement and interest.

3. *Rambling.* Answer only the questions asked of you, not the question you wish you'd been asked. Remember, it's not you running the show. If the interviewer wants to dog the pace, slow up and shut up.

How to Spot an Office Politician

Talk about your Halloween horror: Look in the next cubicle. That smilin' Jack with the curious collection of sharp knives is every working man's nightmare: the back-stabber.

Guys who smile at your face while they wait for you to turn your back are not just jerks. They're passive-aggressive jerks. Here are the signs of the basic model double-dealer:

- *Plays dumb to hide resentment.*
- *Weasels out of promises.*
- *Agrees with you* when you're face-to-face, but disses you to your boss or coworkers.
- *Keeps a low profile* while a tough project is under way, then emerges at the end to share the credit.

The solution? If the guy's your subordinate, face him down. If he's a coworker, cover your butt. If he's your boss, quit.

How to Hook Up with a Mentor

When it comes to sailing the crazy sea of careers, mentors hold the wheel. Everybody needs one. So go out and get one. Then pay attention, because the next mentor may be you.

- *Browsing for a mentor isn't easy.* There are a million would-be mentors out there, guys with 800 numbers and camps in the woods where you can be mentored inside out. By and large, most mentors are modest men. They don't offer a course in miracles or a better way to love the inner you.

- *Mentors also aren't always your father.* Fathers are the working models we use to determine how we're doing as a man, how well we're measuring up to the big job. After all, fathers, either by their accomplishments or by their lack thereof, show us what we need to do to meet a wide range of responsibilities and thereby acquire manly virtues. But the ability of any given dad to mentor is dependent entirely on the subject at hand. Sometimes, in fact, you want to be able to count on your father to duck out of the loop and hook you up with a good mentor when circumstance calls for it. Smart pops know that mentors are often given a more utilitarian role: They don't have enforcement powers of the papa police, and they don't have to worry about paying the bills for your misspent youth. They are instead expected to combine a relatively small sphere of practical advice within a useful moral framework.

For instance, the first mentor—named, conveniently, Mentor—was the aged, trusted adviser with whom Odysseus left his son, Telemachus, when he went off to fight the Trojan War. He made that decision not based on Mentor's baby-sitting abilities. Instead, Odysseus figured Mentor would be able to give Telemachus enough useful information—both applied and theoretical—that, given the example of manly virtues he had set for his son, he could reasonably expect the boy to someday meet or exceed his own expectations for himself. Odysseus knew that a mentor can help you succeed in life sufficiently that you can eventually meet your old man on somewhat equal terms.

How to Buy and Sell Anything

In these disputatious, fractious, ill-spirited times, we know there are a million ways of dividing the planet in two. There's the North-South thing, just for starters. There are haves and have-nots, men and women, owners and players, First World and Third World. Finally, you've got what we can call the OPEC duality: buyers and sellers. And that's where life on earth gets tricky—and expensive. We're buyers some of the time. We're sellers some of the time. And a man needs to be mindful which is which.

Virtually every meeting between a buyer and a seller leaves behind a residue of resentment. Who knows why. It's not that sellers are carnivores in a world of vegan buyers, or that those with money have bludgeoned those with goods. The real problem is that very few people know how to sell anything, and too many people are ready to buy anything. That's why unscrupulous sellers are called "sharks," and why nitwit buyers are called "fish." Which brings us to this useful aphorism:

The angling angle: Everything a good salesman needs to know he can learn by figuring out how to catch a fish.

THE PARTS OF A SALE

When salesmen go to sales school, they learn that every sale has just four ingredients:

1. *Discovery.* When you listen to what the customer wants.
2. *Presentation.* When you offer to supply what the guy says he needs.
3. *Close.* When you shake on it.
4. *Follow-through.* When you call the next week to see how everything's going.

When we want to sell something, most of us have almost no interest in the discovery and follow-through parts, because we know what we want to sell, and we don't particularly care how it works out later. But we go crazy on the presentation and the close. Watch some chap in full courtship mode. He meets a woman, says hello, but can barely bring himself to listen to her name before he starts playing the endless tape of his life. The presentation part of his sale goes on forever. He's thinking that if he can just pitch the product the right way, the closer will take care of itself. Follow-through? Yeah. Sure. He'll call in the morning. Most of us sell cars, houses, garage junk all the same way.

EARS ARE A SALESMAN'S BEST TOOL

Ever notice how some guys can sell anything? We like to think that guys who can sell anything do their work by talking fast and slick. But that's not how it works at all. **Guys who are great salesmen use their ears, not their jaws,** because they know that of all four parts of a sale, it's the listening part that counts most. A good salesman listens to as much as the seller wants to tell him. For example, let's say you're the manager of your local hardware emporium and some suburban gentleman walks in looking for a snowblower. If you're any good, you'll spend the first few minutes listening, maybe asking a few questions: Gas or electric? Hilly lot or level? Macadam driveway or gravel? Because you know if you sell the guy the new General Dynamics Desert Storm snowblower, when what he really needs is the McDonnell Douglas turbo-charged Sno-Sluice Deluxe, you'll have made an enemy. Buyers want guidance and help, not shortcuts.

Besides, *there are added benefits to listening.* Two to be exact: *First, it makes the buyer want you to succeed* in selling him, since you seem to be on the same side, and everybody loves a good listener. *Second, it makes the buyer do the heavy-lifting part of the sale.* Get the buyer to talk to you long enough, and he'll tell you what he needs, why he needs it, and how much. You, the salesman, just have to sit back and write up the order. (A *side tip:* To get a compulsive talker to clam up, start talking about yourself. Works every time, usually within three minutes.)

HOW TO BE A BUYER

There are no schools for buyers as there are for sellers. But if there were, they'd teach the same routine, starting with the importance of listening. If you listen to the salesman, you'll better understand what he's selling and why, and you can make a better deal. Some principles:

- *Find out what's in it for him.* The more the salesman needs the sale, the more likely he'll give you a better price. When you go into a car dealership, you'll know you're in the right place when you see the sales chart showing your salesman is only one sale away from beating out all the other salesmen. The lesson? Go on the last day of the selling period—and that usually means the last day of the month.

- *Be ready to walk.* If the salesman has really listened to you talk about what you want, why you want it, and how you plan to use it, he knows whether or not he's got a sale. It's what happens next that counts. Some salesmen won't try to sell you something you've already said you don't need. But most will. The chance that you'll leave angry is one many salesmen are willing to take. After all, once you're out the door, what difference does it make? Car dealerships, especially, often see a sale in terms of conflict rather than cooperation. Look for a salesman who's willing to work with you, instead of against you; he's the kind of guy who sees his customers as long-term investments, rather than short-term pony-shots.

- *Listen to yourself.* If you expect the salesman to listen to you, you ought to expect the same from yourself. If what you hear is a slight murmur of ambivalence, duck out of the deal until you've had time to think it over. By the way, if a salesman tries to tell you the deal is now-or-never, it's always never. Always.

- **Make the salesman talk.** Just as the salesman gains an edge by listening, the buyer can gain an edge by refusing to talk. Zen-inspired salesmen call this the "Trick of Silence," in which you don't volunteer information, you don't explain conflicting data, you just follow the sort of admonition once given by the smartest man in the world, the late rare-book expert George Leinwall, to a rookie bibliophile attending his first book auction: "Keep your hands in your pockets and your mouth shut."

Now, that doesn't mean you lie, exactly. It just means that you make the seller come to you.

You say, "How much?"

The salesman says, "Twelve-fifty."

And you say nothing. Eventually, the salesman will either say, "Twelve," or say, "So long."

The Trick of Silence works because, just as nature abhors a vacuum, so do natural-born talkers feel compelled to fill any silence. The result is that you get to listen to a lot more than the salesman really intended to tell you. Another example: You say, "How's that car running?" The salesman says, "Fine." You say nothing. Eventually he'll say, "There was a minor accident, but don't you worry. We've repaired the crack in the frame." Keep not talking and eventually you'll learn about the bubble in the tires, the rust on the muffler, and the stains on the backseat. Then, price is up to you.

- **Don't buy the salesman.** Most people instinctively like a good listener. Good salesmen are very good listeners. If a salesman does listen, it's only for purposes of obtaining information. It doesn't mean he likes you.

This is also how men find themselves in alliances with women who are often much smarter than they are. Remember our small scenario, in which some guy is letting the hot air out of the gaseous epic of his life while the woman he's with waits patiently, occasionally counting ceiling tiles? Do you know which party is doing the selling in that situation? The one talking? Or the one listening?

MANNERS AT WORK

Work is where manners assume really huge dimensions of hypocrisy, simply because a failure to be polite at a critical moment can spell the difference between continuing to spend your days at your place of employment and spending them in your basement rec room.

How to Be Nice to Your Boss Without Appearing to Kiss His Ass

It all depends on how honest you are with yourself. If you really do want to brownnose, get an adjustable ball cap with a toilet-paper dispenser mounted on the bill. There's no proper etiquette for brownnosing, but nothing anybody says will stop you. On the other hand, if you think simply being nice, honest, a hard worker, and so forth, will be mistaken for brownnosing, you're making a rude mistake. **Be as nice to the boss as he is to you,** and you'll be golden, etiquettewise.

How to Work for Somebody Who Was Once Your Subordinate

You can't, and to try to do so only puts an impolite burden on your new honcho. Some management decisions carry such an unmistakable subtext that only a desperate fool will ignore the message. Do we have to spell it out? Your name is mud in this company. That said, **this is a situation in which simple rules of good manners will stand you in good stead.** Go to your new boss and tell her you wish her well, that you'll be leaving in a month or so, and that you want to do everything you can before you skedaddle to make sure everything goes smoothly for her. Then do what you said you'd do, *especially including the skedaddle part.* You'll at least leave with a nice reference and a friend, where you could have left an enemy.

How to Deal with a Backstabbing Coworker

Biz-betrayal is everywhere. Let's say you had a brilliant idea, shared it with the guy in the next cubicle, and now's he's getting a raise on the strength of it. What do you do?

Sometimes the rules of etiquette exist not to make others feel at ease, but to make sure we don't hurt ourselves. This is such a scenario. So,

- ***Don't make a big, embarrassing fuss.*** The rude route, when you discover that you've been looted, is to write a memo outlining your claims, send it to your boss, who has already gone out on a limb for your rival, and ask him to see that justice is done. It's not going to happen, first of all, and second, you'll probably be asked rudely to leave.

- ***Since you can't lick 'em, join 'em.*** The polite thing to do is also the sensible thing to do: Go to your idea-grubbing competitor, whom you rightly despise, and sign on to help him make the idea work as well as possible. Be his biggest supporter and his right-hand man. Be loyal and trustworthy, especially trustworthy. One of two things eventually will happen: Since he's operating at a creative level higher than that to which he could rightfully aspire, there's a good chance smoke will eventually spew from his engines, oil will streak along his wings, and he'll crash and burn, at which time you should politely stand aside so as not to be struck by flying debris. That's one thing that might happen. The other thing is that you'll come up with another brilliant idea, and this time you'll guard it wisely and well and with polite persistence until you can implement it to your own credit.

MONEY MANNERS

Money is dirty. Filthy. Essential. It's also inherently mannerless and the root of all bad manners. Some people will sell their friendships, their moms, and their souls if the price is right; these guys love money dearly and are never offended by it. On the other hand, the very existence of money on the same physical plane can be an affront to a polite guy. The result is that whenever you're dealing with money, you're working outside the envelope of etiquette, like a spacewalk, where special protective measures are required for survival.

How to Ask for a Raise

In a polite world, it would never be necessary to ask for a raise. It would be politely offered. The boss would knock softly on your cubicle frame and say, "Sorry, Withers. Do you have a sec? The chairman of the board wondered if it would be inconvenient if we slipped a few extra grand into your pay packet. I mean, if that's okay. If it's no trouble." And you would nod, say, "Yes, of course, Mr. Murdoch, very kind," and there would be no further discussion about something so utterly distasteful. But since we live on Rude World, a man's got to ask. The rules of politely begging for money are these:

- **Be reasonable.** Know what you're worth. A raise is not a right; it's not something granted as a matter of course every few months or years. In fact, you're rude if you ask for a raise simply because nobody's got around to firing you; seniority may be either a mark of your competence or a testament to your employer's humanity. But if you know what you contribute, and you know what that contribution's worth, and if that's not what you're getting, say so in as straightforward a manner as possible. The perfectly phrased raise request comes disguised as an astute observation: "You know, chief, last year I saved the firm three mill, yet I'm getting ten grand less than the other kids. I figure I'm worth more than those guys, and a lot more than what I'm getting now."

- **Be sensible.** You must time a raise request with an awareness of what's going on around you. If the firm has just lost its biggest client, laid off half the force, or had its assets seized by the feds, your request for a raise may strike your boss as being a trifle insensitive, and he may wish to politely trash your behind. The best time to ask for a raise is soon after you or your department has obviously earned it by making a visible and obvious contribution to the company's good fortunes.

- **Be prepared.** There's a good chance any sensible, reasonable request for additional salary might be declined. Refusing to give a man a raise when he's clearly entitled to one and when circumstances obviously permit it is an unambiguous statement from management about one of two things. It means the boss is greedy. Or that you're despised. Either way, the sign you should be looking for reads "Exit." Accept this calmly and politely, and the next day, start a well-planned, deliberate, and overtly civil search for somebody else you can ask for a raise.

5. Trouble and Fun

Most men avoid trouble assiduously only if it comes in unattractive packaging. Put a load of trouble under the hood of a red sports car or in a tight, black dress, though, and trouble becomes our collective middle name. Then we go blind. Why? Because even if it walks like trouble, talks like trouble, and looks like trouble, it looks like fun to us.

Alas, the line between fun and self-destruction isn't even a fine one. It's a four-foot-wide stripe painted in tears, whatever those are.

How to Prevent a Hangover

If you ate cheeseburgers for breakfast every day for a week, you're ready for these handy hints, for curing a hangover is what you must do when you fail to prevent one. To do that:

- **Drink an eight-ounce glass of water** for *every* drink you drank just before you go to bed—and don't cheat.
- **Then pack some carbohydrates** to take along on Slumberland's Tilt-a-Whirl. Bread works.

Neither of these are easy things to do when you're stumbling around the kitchen drunk, but doing both is a lot easier than waking up with a hangover.

- **Try fifty milligrams of vitamin B,** eat a piece of bread, and drink two big glasses of water before you go to sleep.
- **Take two or three aspirin,** acetaminophen, or ibuprofen with a couple of glasses of water before you go to sleep.

For some obscure reason, until the recent lounge movement, people under, say, thirty just didn't appreciate the virtue of a well-made martini—unless they'd drunk a dozen. Now a cold martini is a hot item.

Here's how to be the Bond of the bar:

- **Cold start.** Keep your ingredients on ice or in a freezer until you're ready. One option: Mix your martini in a pitcher or large flower vase and chill the thing.

- *To make one from scratch,* pour two fingers—that's four ounces—of gin or vodka in a chilled martini glass. Add just enough vermouth to cover the bottom of the vermouth bottle's cap. Stir gently. Add a couple of olives. If you add those little cocktail onions, your martini becomes a Gibson. If you add a dash of bitters instead of onions, you can call it a Nigroni. Drink six or seven of them, and not only will you not care what they're called, you'll be well on your way to developing a high-concept resolution idea for next year.

How to Cure a Hangover

- *Use science.* You thought it was the booze. Wrong. It was the chemistry: That mixed cocktail of misbehavior dehydrated your body, nauseated your stomach, and beat you up alongside the head. So fight chemistry with chemistry: Drink plenty of—do we have to say it? *nonalcoholic*—liquids, eat something savory to help retain water, and give your body a good dose of protein. One man's prescription: double cheeseburger, large fries, huge cola with ice. And that's for *breakfast,* chum.
- *Eat a dry cracker with honey on it* if you feel bad when you wake up.
- *Take one thousand milligrams of vitamin C,* drink salted cucumber juice, eat raw fish marinated in hot sauce, and take ginseng or willow bark.
- *Eat tomatoes,* drink V-8 and coffee, and take a cold shower.
- *Drink lots of water* and ginger root tea.
- *Exercise.*

How to Swallow a Sword

First, you have to swallow a guiding tube, which is generally seventeen to nineteen inches long and less than an inch wide and made of thin metal. This tube will protect your throat from the sword's sharp edges.

So, the real question is: How do you swallow a sword-guiding tube?

- **Start with something small,** a spoon perhaps, to overcome the gag reflex. The greatest danger here, believe it or not, is getting so comfortable with a spoon thrust down your throat that you drop it and—ouch! And ouch, again!
- **Open wide, tilt back, and align the spoon** with your pharynx. That's about five inches down. Now it's time to move up to something a bit longer—a chopstick, perhaps. Past the pharynx easily, and into the esophagus (ten to eleven inches). The idea here is to make a straight line from your mouth to your stomach.
- **Now use the guiding tube as a practice instrument.** The last door to pass through is the distended stomach. When you get there, you're ready for a real sword.

How to Organize a Friendly Little Poker Game

What we have here is your basic euphemistic oxymoron, since there is no such thing as a "friendly" poker game. There may exist a poker game played by people all of whom are friends. But poker is quiet war; it's tidy bloodlust; it's ripping the guts out of the guy next to you and tossing them back in his face with a pair of aces. Unless, of course, you let women play and use wild cards. In which case poker is a card game.

Regularly-scheduled poker nights have something slightly institutional about them; they acquire traditions and eccentricities that somehow make them different from all other poker games. Partly, that's personnel; partly that's

- **Location:** Probably one player's home. It's best not to rotate the venue; situating the game more or less permanently in one place reinforces the notion that the game is a regular, unchanging thing.

- *Primarily poker:* The venue should be dedicated to poker for the night. Mixing poker with your wife's Tupperware party somehow denigrates the intrinsic importance of The Game.
- *Facilities and materials:* Good lighting, enough chairs, a practically proportioned table, plenty of ashtrays, a mess of red, blue, and white chips, and four decks of cards—two red, two blue—are standard.
- *Refreshments:* There are two ways to share food duty: Either one person is *always* responsible, or the winner is responsible for bringing food the following week. If you choose the former option, rake a buck from each pot until the tab is paid.

A limited supply of beer is okay, but avoid hard stuff. Poker is best played with a straight face.

- *Players:* Seven is ideal; five or six will do. Never play a four-handed game. The best way to ensure a steady supply of players is to find five or six regulars, leaving one or two chairs open for guests. That way, if a regular becomes irregular, he can be demoted to guest, and a guest can be elevated to regular. Boot chronic no-shows.

Try and exercise some demographic sense in picking your players: If your group includes three guys on student loans and three neurosurgeons, odds are you'll have a short and uninteresting game.

- *Stakes:* The stakes and limits are probably the most important elements in a regular game. The stakes should be high enough to mean something—ever try and bluff your way into an eighty-cent pot?—but not so high that some guy's kids won't be able to eat. A quarter or a half-dollar seems to work pretty well for most people, especially if you limit raises to three.
- *House rules:* House or game rules should be sensible and easy to remember, and they should be made clear to everyone before the very first hand of the very first game is played. Newcomers should always have house rules explained to them. Remember that the object of house rules is to ensure fair play in a congenial atmosphere.

Here's a decent list of house rules:

Maximum three-dollar initial bet with a three-raise, three-dollar-per-raise maximum.

No check-and-raise betting.

Ties split the pot.

No wild cards, and no games that require more cards than the table can supply (i.e., in a seven-man game, no eight-card games).

A card laid is a card played.

Hoyle's Rules of Poker is *the judge.*

- **Games:** Stick with games everyone knows. Esoteric games with lots of blind flips, wild cards, extra buys, and passes are social games, not poker games, and usually find favor only when the game is thoroughly co-ed. For a good, smooth game, stick to draw and stud games and their variants. Adding high-low splits can liven up a game.

- **Duration:** Set a quitting time and *stick to it.* If you have a mid-week game that starts at seven, call for a last deal around the table at, say, midnight.

- **Clean up:** Either everybody pitches in, or the winners clean up and the losers are excused. But never ask your girlfriend or wife to do janitor duty, since if you do, there's a very good chance your first poker game will be your last.

- **If you're invited** to someone else's game, learn the house rules, try and gain at least a superficial acquaintance with the other players, and stay until the end. Ask the person inviting you what the stakes are; if they're too high for you, don't go.

HOW TO INJECT PURE FEAR INTO A FRIENDLY, LITTLE POKER GAME

A personal observation: A Mr. F. W. of Los Angeles wrote to me asking about weird poker games: "Is there one particular card game that's more exciting than any others? I'm looking for something to really shake up my regular group." That's an odd question to ask from L.A. Just call for a quick round of earthquakes.

If you're looking for a scary card game, there's a certain charming terror in any poker game in which you are the regular loser. In fact, I used to be part of a weekly poker game in Hollywood in which I played just that role. The other regulars—agents, writers, actors—were all rich, and I did what I could to help them stay that way. I played every Wednesday for five years, and I lost the equivalent of a new Toyota every year. I was actually pretty fair at conventional games—stud, draw, all those. The economic stimulus I gave the nation was from a brutal, barbaric game without a name, but based on one much more civilized called "Bourée," a word which in French means, "Your money or your wife."

Here's how you make it hurt:

- *Ante a buck.*
- *Deal four cards facedown to everyone.*
- *Turn up one card from somewhere in the middle of the deck. That's your tramp suit; aces are high. Bury that card and shuffle.*
- *One betting round. Here's what you're betting: You're betting that you can take at least one trick of the four tricks that will be played.*
- *Then the first declaration: Play or fold?*
- *If you play, you can replace any number of cards for a dollar each.*
- *If you fold, you're not only out of the hand but out of the game.*
- *Another betting round.*
- *Second declaration: Play or fold?*
- *If you play and manage to take just one, little, lousy trick, all you have to do to stay in for the next round is ante another buck.*
- *If two players tie at two tricks each, they each ante a buck.*
- *If you take all the tricks, you take the pot.*

- *But—and, really, this is the unpleasant part—if you take no tricks, you match the pot.*

  This ugly exercise continues, round after round, until every player but one folds. At a table of seven players, I'm willing to bet your hands will shake so hard you won't be able to hold your cards during the last round. This monstrosity is the spinal tap and root canal of all poker games. Give it a name and let me know what you decide. "Testicular Cancer" might work.

How to Spot a Cold Dealer

There is such a thing as a cold dealer in twenty-one. When you spot one, make sure you sit down and get in the game. Here's what he looks like:

Watch the hands he deals himself. If he shows a 2, 3, 4, 5, or 6 in five out of ten hands, make him a friend for life—or at least until the cards change.

Here's why: If he's got a 2 to 6 showing, odds are he's got a high card underneath. Since he has to hit anything under 17, the odds are still in favor of him getting another high card, thus going bust.

Keep in mind that the rule may also be true for you: If you get a 2, 3, 4, 5, or 6 in five hands out of ten, it might be time for you to get out of the game.

More gambling wisdom:

- *Believe in streaks.* They can be proven statistically. Therefore, stay when you're on a good one, split when you're not.
- *Pick the right game.* At a casino, the game with the best odds in your favor (if you know what you're doing) is blackjack. The worst odds are the slots.
- *Don't play the state lottery.* But if you must, play in Virginia, where the odds are the best.

How to Post Bail

First, you have to qualify. If the judge thinks your crime is too awful or that you seem likely to try to escape the court's jurisdiction, you may be sent to jail to wait for your trial.

But *if the judge feels that you are trustworthy enough* to be let free until your trial, he will require that you put some money up front to assure you won't fly the coop before the trial is over. The money will be returned to you when you show up as promised.

- *If the money is more than you keep lying around,* you'll have to go to a bail bondsman. How to find one? Don't worry: Their cards and signs will be everywhere around you. In exchange for collateral or a fee that will begin at about 10 percent, the bail bondsman will pay your fee to the court. The amount of the collateral or fee will vary according to how likely the bail bondsman feels you are to jump bail or disappear before your trial is over.

- *If you fail to appear* in court as ordered after having your bail posted, you will have compounded whatever problems you were already having. The court will file charges against you for jumping bail; you will lose whatever fee you paid or collateral you posted to the bondsman. And what's worse, you will have an angry bondsman on your tail. Chances are, given his line of work, he's got all kinds of friends who know how to take care of guys like you.

How to Negotiate a Late-Night Re-entry

Circumstances: Out late misbehaving. Woman home in bed.

- *Objective:* Silent re-entry.
- *Obstacles:* Unexpected objects on floor, creaking floorboards, squeaky binges.
- *Solution:* Unlock the door making as much noise as you wish. Run inside, turn on the TV. When your significant other comes downstairs to ask what's up, tell her you fell asleep in front of the TV and thought you heard a racket at the door.
- *Alternate:* Take off your clothes, unlock the door, run inside, pile clothes next to sofa, claim you decided to sleep on the sofa because she had taken all the blankets—never pass up a chance for guilt manipulation—but that you were awakened by a racket at the door.

- *Caution:* The alternate plan is so outrageous that it usually works. There is a slight risk, however, in the doorstep strip, so plan carefully in case you have to dive into the shrubbery.

And if your wife or girlfriend is sitting quietly reading by the fire when you rush in, naked, and pop on the TV?

- *Watch out for crafty women:* The danger is with all that stuff they make and over-decorate the house with. For example, baskets of pine cones on the floor, cluttered-up bathroom fixtures, arrangements of dried leaves—these things are all distant early-warning devices designed to catch an unwary prodigal spouse.

How to Move a Bees' Nest

- *First, pick the right day*—a warm sunny one—when the bees are already in a good mood.
- Next, *rent a smoke-blowing unit* and use it to encourage the bees to leave the hive. The smoke makes them bee-drunk and passive.
- *Wear light-colored clothing* with a smooth finish—like polished cotton or khaki—and protect your face and neck with a bee veil.
- *Wear boots* and loose-fitting gloves that seal well around the wrists and your shirt collar.
- *Tie your trousers* shut at the leg.

Once you have the nest in hand, move slowly and confidently. Exhibit no fear or nervousness. The bees will sense it.

How to Survive a Towering Inferno

- *Go to the door* of your room and feel it with your hand—but don't open it! If it is hot, leave it closed. If it is cool, open it and see how much smoke is in the hallway.
- *Check for smoke.* If there is little or none, leave your room and go to the emergency stairwell. Do not use the elevator.
- *Make sure you take your room key* with you. If the stairwell is filled with smoke or flames, you many need to retreat back to your room.

- ***Block the door.*** If the door of your room is hot or there is heavy smoke in the hallway, wet some towels and put them along the base of the door to keep the smoke out. Remember: Smoke kills most victims of fire, not flames.
- ***Move to the window*** or balcony with sheet in hand. If you have a balcony, close the door behind you. If you have a fear of heights, turn and face the wall.
- ***If you can't get out, get air.*** If the room has narrow windows you can't fit through, put a wet towel over your head and get low to suck in the fresh air coming in the window.
- ***Wind direction.*** If your room doesn't have a balcony, determining the direction of the wind is crucial: If the wind is blowing toward you, you can open the window as wide as you like. But if the wind is blowing away from you and you open the window, you will create a vacuum in the room and the fire and smoke may come rushing in to fill it. If the wind is blowing away from you, don't open the window any more than three inches. The same rules apply to windows that are sealed: If the wind is blowing toward you, break the window. If the wind is blowing away from you, do nothing.
- ***One last tip.*** Whether you are in a hotel or at home, it is always a good idea to sleep with your shoes at the side of the bed. Why? In

the event of fire or earthquake or other disaster, window glass may break and fall on the floor, waiting to cut an unsuspecting and barefoot victim. Besides, you may have to do a little fire-walking to get away safely.

How to Duck an IRS Audit

To successfully avoid an audit, you must first know the mind of the IRS. Here's the meld:

- *An audit is not an accusation* of wrongdoing. It's just an audit.
- *All returns are run through a computer,* which checks the math and flags returns with errors. At the same time, the computer also flags returns with high deductions at each income level. The higher your income, the more likely you are to be audited. Also, people who live in large cities are more likely to be audited.
- *Flagged returns are then examined by a human,* who decides whether an audit is warranted or not.
- Ergo, *the best (but not foolproof) way to avoid an audit* is to keep your deductions within the range that is considered "normal" for someone of your marital status and income level. However, don't get smug if you do this: A certain number of "normal" returns are randomly selected and audited each year.
- Meanwhile, *having an unusually high deduction doesn't guarantee that you will be audited,* either, so the best thing to do is to report your income and deductions honestly, and make sure you can document everything you are deducting.
- *Hold on to those slips of paper:* The IRS can audit you for any or all of the past three years.

How to Survive an IRS Audit

- *It's okay to be pleasant,* but don't try to be obsequious.
- *Don't try to* make the examiner like you.
- *When you feel like talking* to fill in the silences, don't.

- **Don't yammer.** Briefly, politely, and succinctly answer the question asked, nothing more.
- **Don't get angry** or complain or threaten to write your congressman—the examiner is only doing his job. Being pleasant may not hurt (and it could help), but getting angry certainly won't help.
- **Bring every piece of documentation** necessary to answer the examiner's queries.

How to Deal with Fear

Perhaps one of the most well-trod lines in American political speech-making is FDR's claim that we have nothing to fear but fear itself. FDR is obviously not a man who ever skidded broadside across the width of the Pennsylvania Turnpike heading directly at the big, white underbelly of a gasoline truck.

The fears of a normal man. FDR, as it happens, wasn't talking fear at all, as any sensible fellow can attest. He was pitching a get-up-and-get-going, don't-worry-be-happy cheerfulness to the nation when it was in a state of severe depression. What Roosevelt meant by "fear" was really something a little closer to defeatism, a thing to be avoided, no doubt, but hardly the kind of thing that makes your hair stand on end. If FDR really wanted to take the fear out of fear, he should have at least been talking about the fears we all know and, well, fear. Here's a fearful little list:

1. **Fear of dropping the ball.** Literally. You're sitting with your kid in a box behind third, Rube fouls one off. The ball comes right at you, your kid yells, "Catch it, Dad!" and you feel your hands turn to mush. The problem, of course, is that most men wilt under too much carefully observed pressure. That's why public speaking is a big fear.

2. **Fear of dancing.** Lots of guys are afraid of dancing, because the moment they get out on the dance floor, they have an out-of-body experience, in which they see themselves as Al Gore frugging to "Don't Stop Thinking About Tomorrow," and nearly lose their

will to live. Usually, guys who want to dance but fear the sight of themselves dancing have to drink so much to work up nerve enough to take a turn that when they stand to rumba, they fall over.

3. *Fear of beautiful women.* Most middle-aged women think men are terrified of smart, strong, independent women. That's nonsense, of course. Men love smart, ambitious women, since they're exactly the kind of women who will work hard enough to make sure we all get plenty of time for golf. No, men are terrified of beautiful, *young* women. There are a number of ways men mask this fear. The most common method is by cranking up their level of testosteronal boorishness and behaving rudely toward a good looking woman, so that when her inevitable rebuff comes, these guys can attribute it to something other than their intrinsic undesirability. Men know beautiful women can be wooed only with an arsenal of wit, charm, civility, and, in distant fourth place, attractiveness—or, occasionally, their cash equivalents—and no man wants to admit he's lacking in these respects. As we all know, smart, strong, independent, not-so-great-looking women can be won with a combination of good hair and a lascivious smolder.

4. *Fear of asbestos in the basement.* It's a planet of radon out there, in which every day we find a new secret killer in our midst, a silent, insidious terror against which only really expensive experts can protect us. The experts, of course, tell us that there are invisible killers everywhere, spreading cancer and strep and HIV. Trouble is, they're right.

5. *Fear of changing the oil.* There are many, many things of which a man is capable but which he chooses not to do by simply saying, "I don't get it." Here's a short list: Taxes, fatherhood, engine maintenance, macroeconomics, nutrition, religion, and multiplication of fractions. Once we agree that all these things are mastered by people of quite ordinary intellect, people even dumber than us, we have to admit that we, too, could do any or all of them, except *we don't want to.*

6. *Fear of dentistry.* This is the only fear that fits the dictionary definition of fear—as anxiety caused by the possibility of danger. Just

thinking about a guy with a hangover drilling holes in your head is enough to give pause to the most fearless of stout hearts. In fact, as most dentists will tell you, it's the fear that gives their patients the willies, not the actual thing—excruciating pain—feared. Most people get in and out of dental chairs with no untoward incidents, other than the sheer misery of being there.

7. **Fear of Sam Bohn.** Sam Bohn represents the guy in your town who owns the local bank. Nice guy, a tennis nut, but you owe him a lot of money. That makes him your inspiration, for it's our incessant fear of creditors that keeps us on the run, workwise, because we're rightly afraid of what they'll do to us if we take a day off. No money means no control. *Boo!* Very scary. So there they are, the magnificent seven of fear: Failure, ridicule, rejection, death, responsibility, pain, and powerlessness.

SITUATIONAL AND OTHER FEARS

You'll notice many phobias missing from the above list. Fear of flying, fear of drunks in trucks, fear of homicidal crossing guards—all these things are fears, real enough. But I don't think anybody not insane is really living in fear of these things. That is, you get scared of them when they're around, that's all. Otherwise, you never give them a thought.

Other fears are so big you can barely see them, let alone worry about them. Take the wrath of God, for example. It's there, like a tiny leak in a basement pipe. You know you should worry about it, but you get busy and forget it. Then one day you're face-to-face with a flooded basement. Damn!

HOW TO PACIFY YOUR OWN FEARS

Had FDR said, "We have nothing to fear but ridicule, rejection, pain, and death," the nation would *still* be down in the dumps. Ironically, Roosevelt was right about the cure, wrong about the fear. What FDR needed was a good spin on the Cyclone at Coney Island. It would have made all fears comprehensible to him.

Here's how you can cope with fear: Take the thing you're most afraid of—impoverishment, for example—and spend some time developing a whole scenario based on what could *conceivably* happen to you if, to use our example, joblessness came your way. Work out all the details—all the conversations with friends, all the snide remarks of enemies. Get it all down. Live it. Survive it. Then get back on your feet and try again. A little fear is a useful thing, so long as it's a know-it-and-love-it kind of deal. That's the very thing that makes roller coasters so attractive: You get to *almost* die. See? Roller coasters are to death what sex is to love. That's why roller coasters are so much more popular than actually dying.

And, on that cheerful subject, a poll taken several years ago reported that 2 percent of respondents were willing to take a 99 percent chance of dying for one million dollars. Scary, no?

HOW TO SIZE UP A CIGAR

The larger the diameter of the cigar—measured in cigar-ring sizes—the richer and fuller the taste. The longer the cigar, the cooler the taste.

Know the parts:

- *Wrapper:* The outer tobacco wrapping, which ranges in color from light to very dark (called "oscuro").
- *Binders:* The layer of tobacco just beneath the wrapper. It's used to hold all the filler tobacco in the center together.
- *Filler:* The tobacco at the center of the cigar. This is the stuff you're really smoking. There are two kinds of filler:
  Long filler: Runs the length of the cigar
  Short filler: Comes from the trimmed edges of the long fillers. A high percentage of short filler is undesirable.

How to Blow a Smoke Ring

- *You don't need a weatherman.* If there's any wind at all, no ring.
- *Fill your mouth completely with smoke.* You need not a wisp, but a billow.

- **Slowly open your lips** to form a perfect "O." Not a pucker, and not a yawn. An "O." A perfect one. Bring those lips over those teeth. Come on. An "O." No other vowel will do. In Poland, smoke rings are an impossibility, owing to a linguistic shortfall in vowels. But in Hawaii, where vowels grow wild, there are smoke rings everywhere.
- **Push the tip of your tongue down** into the fleshy spot behind your lower front teeth, and pull the rest of your tongue as far back into your mouth as you can. Raise your chin slightly.
- One way is to **push the smoke out of your mouth with your tongue**. Try it. Okay, try the other way:
- **Keep that "O" on your lips, and try to close your mouth.** You'll feel a sort of click as your jaw tries to do the impossible. You'll create just enough of a contraction to send a ring aloft.

Note that you don't actually "blow" a smoke ring. In fact, if you exhale while trying to blow a ring, you'll create too much of a draft. Instead of blowing a ring, you sort of *push* one.

How to Land a Big Rig

Say, frequent fliers, here's a trouble clip n' save for that next time you hear the dreaded announcement over the intercom: "Ladies and gentlemen, there's been an accident in the cockpit. Is there anybody on board who knows how to land a 747?"

Boeing 747s are wonderful airplanes. But they're real huge; the late, great Michael O'Donoghue once suggested making a matchbook advertising a study-at-home course called "Learn to Fly the Big Rigs." Well, this isn't the whole matchbook study plan, but it's the part that counts:

1. **First, admit you have a problem.** Grab the radio and tell anybody who'll listen that you're at the stick of a 747 and you aren't quite sure what to do. While you're waiting for acknowledgment and instructions, go on to step two.
2. **Engage a single channel of the autopilot**—you'll see three buttons marked "CMD." You want to light only one button. Point the heading indicator in the direction so you can keep the airplane

straight and level. A 747 weighs a lot. The last thing you want to do is wrestle with it. Now you've got some time to get organized.

3. ***Find the checklists.*** The landing checklists and cards are always in the side pocket next to the pilot's and copilot's seats. The checklists will tell you if you're landing a 747-400 or another type of 747. If it turns out that you're bringing in a 747-400, you're in luck, since this model is equipped with an automatic landing system (ALS). If it turns out to be another type of 747, see below under "How to Land When There's No ALS."

4. **If you can't find the checklists,** use the three that follow. They're for a British Airways 747-136/236, checklist, and while other companies and types of 747s have different lists, these are better than no lists at all.

   1. ***Before descent checklist:***
      A. The EO's system check should be *completed.*
      B. Pressurization should be *set.*
      C. All a/c packs *on.* Set the airfield altitude so that the aircraft is depressurized on landing. (See below under "Find the Jeppeson.")
      D. Humidifier *off.* You'll still sweat, don't worry.
      E. Landing data and limits: *Checked and set.* This means you've reviewed the data for landing.
      F. HSIs: *Radio.* Switch the horizontal situation indicators to radio navigation mode.
      G. Approach briefing: *Understood.* Now here's where things can get confusing, since normally there would be a full and comprehensive briefing by the landing pilot, but since that's you, well, skip it.
      H. Auto brakes: *Set.* This optimistic step will turn on the automatic braking on touchdown.

   2. ***Approach checklist:***
      A. P.A. call ("Cabin crew fifteen minutes to landing"): *Done.*
      B. Cabin signs and exit lights: *On.*
      C. Ignition: *On.* This will switch on all engine igniters for landing.
      D. Fuel system: *Set for landing.*

  E. Fuel heat (only on 747-136 aircraft): *Check/off,* to prevent fuel icing.

  F. Q.N.H.: *Set.* This is for the altimeter barometric setting that will make the altimeters read the airfield altitude on touchdown.

 3. ***Landing checklist:***

  A. *Gear check: Down, in, green.* In other words, the gear handle is down, the gear handle is in, and the green gear-down lights are on.

  B. Speedbrake: *Armed.* Speedbrakes deploy on touchdown to reduce the lift on the wing and to keep the aircraft from bouncing down the runway.

  C. Hydraulics: *Checked.*

  D. Landing Flap: *Set*—probably at twenty-five degrees of flap, but thirty in a pinch.

  E. SCCM's report: *Received.* This tells you that the Senior Cabin Crew Member reports that the cabins are all secure for landing.

5. ***Find the Jeppeson.*** While you're running down the checklists, grab the Jeppeson charts. These are big notebook-shaped volumes. Inside are maps and landing approach diagrams for practically every airport in the world. Find the airport you're hoping to reach, and locate its radio frequency. Keep the Jeppeson handy. You'll need it again in a sec.

6. ***Find the flight management system.*** Look for buttons on the mode control panel—mounted on the glareshield—marked "LNAV" and "VNAV."

7. ***Find the airport on the Jeppeson map.*** If the crew had entered the arrival airport and approach information before being raptured, put the map on a one-hundred-mile scale using the EFIS control panel on the front instrument panel. When it is time to descend, there will be a yellow FMC MESSAGE message on the middle screen.

8. ***Next, look down at the control display unit*** mounted in the aisle stand between the pilots' seats. The bottom line will read "Reset MCP Altitude." That's telling you to lower the altitude on the mode control panel. Twist the knob in the direction that makes

the little numbers go lower, and stop at about one hundred feet above the field elevation, as shown in the Jeppeson.

9. ***Get the aircraft set to land.*** Even though it's early, the LOC and G/S buttons on the MCP can be depressed to engage the autoland function. This should make all three autopilot CMD buttons light up. The system will *automatically* tune the appropriate ILS frequency. Cool or what?

10. ***Turn on the autobrakes.*** The autobrake panel location differs between airlines. Right about now, the airplane will have descended to intercept the radio-based landing beam. The autopilot will land the airplane. Forget trying to use thrust reversers. Let the autobrakes do the job.

How to Jump Out of an Airplane

Give up on that 747? Practice your getaway move on something more modestly sized. There are three ways to make that first jump:

1. ***Static line:*** You go alone and—usually—your chute opens automatically just seconds after you leave the plane

2. ***Accelerated free-fall:*** You jump (or get pushed) out of the plane at 10,000 to 12,000 feet with two certified jumpmasters, both of whom keep a grip on you and help you get stable in the air, ... monitor the altitude, and—after free-falling for about 50 seconds— pull the ripcord at about 4,000 feet.

3. ***Tandem jump:*** You and a tandem-master are strapped together for the duration of the jump. The tandem-master wears a really big chute, under which you both free-fall for thirty seconds, then float to the ground.

SOCIAL MANNERS

What to Do If You Cut One

Speaking of bringing something up: If the waiter's news comes as such as shock to you that you actually pass gas, you have a new but somehow related problem. What to do in case of flagrant fragrance?

- *If it's a silent poof, ignore it.* S**t happens, as they say.
- *But if the foghorn in your shorts screams, "Fart alert! Dive! Dive!"* you have to acknowledge its existence in the world. The best way: Deal with it as if it were an unexpected burp. Just say, "Yow. Sorry." Make even less of this than you would about a credit card being denied even though both situations stink.

How to Propose a Formal Toast

Some guys make it look so easy. But standing up in a room full of strangers and talking to a glass of alcohol can be the first step to social oblivion, unless you plan ahead.

- *Don't extemporize.* Reduce what you want to say down to three, maybe four sentences. Then be still.
- *You're funny enough.* Unless you're Billy Crystal, you're going to have to get by on your charm, not your wit. Make your toast friendly and pleasant, not pretentious and not forced.
- *Timing is* everything. So wait until everybody's on hand, and hold off until all the chairs have been pulled in. The principal toast to a guest of honor should come just after everybody has been seated. A toast saying thanks should precede dessert.
- *Speak up.* Clink your fork on your wineglass—softly. Then say what you have to say loud enough for everybody to hear it.
- *Drink up.* Don't dribble.

How to Answer a Friend Who Asks for a Loan

There's no reason money and friendship can't be mixed, provided you observe the rules of friendship, especially in making or requesting a loan. Here's what that means, bottom line: You know your friend, you know how he ticks, you know how he feels about money, women, stocks, baseball. You know he doesn't feel the same way about all these things as you do. But you also know, as a matter of respect, that you're not going to impose your values on him or be able to change his behavior in any big way. So when it comes time to lend or borrow money, you have to evaluate two things: One, how the loan is structured. Two, the dollar value of the friendship. It's not polite to borrow from or lend money to a friend until you do those things first. So,

- *Set the ground rules.* If your pal is an organized guy, normally solvent, temporarily short on cash, but otherwise careful in managing the details of his life, he's probably a guy who sees a loan as a relatively mundane business matter. That means you should both be able to make the loan contingent on a mutually agreed payback date or sequence of payments, including interest if you think that makes sense, and to put it all in writing.

- *Or at least be aware of what you're risking.* If your friend is crazy-wild with women and debts, but that's part of the reason you like him, make the loan with an assumption that you may never see your money again. The friendship, after all, is the only collateral you have, and if your buddy reneges, it's the only thing you can repo.

In both cases, it's as rude to lend more than you can afford to risk as it is to borrow more than you can possibly repay.

See also "How to lend Money to Friends" in Chapter 8.

What to Do If You've Been Left Off a Party List

Last year you got invited to the Party of the Century. This year, you didn't. What do you do? That's easy. You assume it's not a mistake and that she's not your friend anymore, and you forget it. Don't call, don't seek revenge, don't whine to all her friends. **Nothing's more impolite than belaboring the obvious.**

How to Confront People Who Are Bad-mouthing You

Hmm. That brings us to **Main Thing** number two of modern etiquette: When the only polite thing to do in response to rude behavior is itself rude, do it with relish.

- *Tell it like it is.* While it would normally be rude to confront somebody with evidence of his misdeeds, in this case the thing to do is seek to alleviate the discomfort you have obviously caused someone. The way to do that is to ask the guy to his face why he said what he said behind your back. Simple enough, no? Then you can ask what he suggests you do to make him feel better. Do it like this: "I understand you think I pilfer pocket change out of the March of Dimes box at the reception desk." The chump will hem and haw and probably deny it. Don't let it slide; force it out into the open. Ask straight out, "What would make you feel that way?" When the guy says it's because he saw you with your arm up to your elbow in the money jar, you can tell him you were just making change or whatever, but the important thing is you'll have diffused the situation on your own terms. Not only is this direct approach polite, it feels good, too.

- **But don't sabotage your informant.** One caution: This confrontation must not be made at the expense of a third party, so if challenging the miscreant reveals that another friend has shared a confidence or is otherwise tattling, let it go until you get it from at least one other source. Meanwhile, you can take solace in this: Nobody is so thoroughly reviled as a coward, and since bad-mouthing is usually done to obtain favor, it will comfort you to know that it actually has the opposite effect. Therefore, by the time you can seek redress, the gossip has already paid the price of his wickedness.

THE MERITS OF CHEAP FABRICATION

Here's a small list of circumstances in which, generally speaking, lying is essential to survival.

- **Deception against your enemies.** Lying is more than just making stuff up, of course. It's also a matter of not telling the truth when you know it. Sometimes, whole armies lie at once because if they didn't, they'd be truly dead. Stormin' Norman didn't tell Saddam the whole truth in the days leading up to Desert Storm, just as Ike didn't fess up to Hitler that Omaha Beach looked like a nice place for an on-shore, D-Day assault.
- **Lying for medicinal purposes.** The tangled relationship between a doctor and his patient can become a tightly woven lace of lies if the doctor determines that the patient's possession of the truth

would be hazardous to his health. Likewise, we all lie to doctors and—especially—dentists all the time. In revenge they lie right back: "This won't hurt a bit," he said, pushing a Black and Decker right through an upper molar and into your cranium. It should be noted, though, that sometimes the lie of the patient has as much effect on the outcome of an illness as the lie of the doctor; sometimes, only the will of the patient to believe he will live—despite verifiable evidence to the contrary—is all he has to pull him through. When this happens, doctors say, "It's a miracle," while patients say, "I told you so."

Alas, sometimes patients also say "I told you so" after complaining to a doctor they were sick, only to have the doctor assume they were lying—until just after the funeral, when the body goes in and the truth comes out.

- *Lies of social lubrication.* When people ask you how you're doing, they are fervently praying for you to lie, unless you're doing fine, thanks. People ask men on their *deathbeds* how they're doin', and all they want to hear is, "Pretty damned good, considering," or something similar. Here's a scene replayed frequently: The emergency crew shows up to wrestle most of a guy out of a squashed car, and the first thing they ask him is always, "How you doin'?" There's a fifty-fifty chance the guy'll say, "Uh, hanging on," just before he dies, the lie still on his lips.

- *Lies of self-flattery.* Telling ourselves lies is an important ingredient in building self-esteem. There are a number of ways of doing this, but dressing for it is the easiest way. As some of you lads may already know, beneath every cashmere sweater lies the double possibility of a well-upholstered lie. Lies have long been a staple of fashion, of course: The whole business of clothiers is to make us look better than we, in fact, do. But nothing screams "Fiction!" with quite the sincerity of a WonderBra. This may seem trivial, but it's not. If we can't trust our eyes, whom or what can we trust? Only this modest book, alas.

- *Lies forced on us by divine will.* Despite the abundance of deceitful propaganda to the contrary, men are the sex possessing the greatest virtue. For the most part, we work hard, play by the rules, treat women fair and square, and despise rogue males who sully our reputation. But we also love sex, and so we are vulnerable to women who often *strip* of us our honor, *use* us as sexual toys, then *abandon* us to our moral failure. A small example: Your wife shows up at home one day with a haircut like Andre Agassi's, a black ninja-clown suit, and a face from Disney and says, "It's the new me! Do you like it, honey?" Suddenly, you are robbed of your moral armor, stripped of your virtue, cheated out of sinlessness, because your alternative to telling a huge lie—"You look *marvelous!*"—is to fast from the flesh forever. This ultimately defeats the life-giving desire of Nature and therefore is a slap at God. So lie or burn.

- *Lies of labor.* Many men find employment because of their awesome ability to lie. The PR business is rich in accomplished deceivers; the same guys who represented the Kuwaitis to America—remember those hospital slaughters later found to be fakes?—next represented the Bosnians. We used to trust our newspapers not only to tell the truth but to manufacture our wars. But now, nobody in their right mind believes what they read or hear in the media.

But in a larger sense, we are all hired contingent on our willingness to tell a lie when our employer wishes the lie to be the truth. *Telling the truth to your employer is just as difficult as telling the truth to your wife,* even though every boss on the planet says he wants employees who aren't afraid to tell the truth. They all say, "I hate yes men." And their employees all rise as one to say, "Me, too, boss!"

THE WHOLE TRUTH—FAST AND LOOSE

There is a modern conceit in the air that suggests that the truth is a relative thing—that what you see as true is only true for you, and that it may be false for others. This is tolerant enough, but it's also ridiculous, since the truth is one of those things—like bad checks or foam falsies—that are subject to eventual verification.

An example: Women who on the telephone have absolutely fabulous voices.

Understanding that truth is a real thing is critical to understanding a lie. Hell, you can't even lie if there is no objective truth. It's pretty squirrely that we all agree on what constitutes a lie—"I didn't inhale"— easier than we agree on what constitutes the truth—is the guy a pothead? But one's as good as the other when you come right down to it.

This counts, because *lies require heavy maintenance.* You can't just tell a lie and walk away from it. You have to nurture it, prune it, water it, keep looking after it, making sure it doesn't get choked out by the weeds of truth, which is the cosmic volunteer and the ultimate victor. Therefore, when you lie, make sure you know the truth. Otherwise, not only will you add confusion to your already complex life, but you'll never know when you're lying. For examples, consider:

THE DARK SIDE OF LYING

This is the kind of stuff that gives lying a bad name. With these abuses of the truth, harm is done to others, no matter how thoroughly you have worked out your own self-justification.

- **Ideological lies.** The ultimate result of trivializing the truth and making it relative is that the truth is often subordinated in favor of superior virtues. When politicians, bureaucrats, and special-interest pleaders want to achieve a goal—say, the right to a free education by all mammals—they crank out reports, surveys, "findings," and other spurious research designed to create a smooth, synthetic truth suggesting that beavers flourish when exposed to Russian literature or that whales are fine painters, despite the fact that none of it is objectively true. After all, the goal isn't to reveal the truth, but to achieve virtue. It doesn't matter to either the politicians or the media that the virtuous end is a false one, since everybody knows the truth is often far less compelling than self-righteousness.

- **Lies of optimism.** We all tell these teeny whopperettes all the time. Here's how they work: Somebody will ask you to meet him at the corner of State and Main, thirty miles from your house, at noon. According to you, you live five minutes from State and Main. It's right *there,* around that corner and down that road and hang a left. Okay, seven minutes, tops. According to the laws of physics and the Department of Motor Vehicles, however, you live at least thirty minutes away. Nevertheless, even in the face of overwhelming scientific evidence that one cannot drive a conventional automobile the 240 MPH required to actually reach State and Main from your house in the 7 minutes you invariably allot yourself, you remain optimistic that it can be done. So you are always twenty-three minutes late. This causes others distress.

- *Lies of blinding stupidity.* These are the lies we most regret telling—lies that gain us nothing, yet bind us forever to the lie we've told. Entire Presidential administrations have been shaped by lies of this variety.

- *Lies of aspiration.* These are the lies you tell because you think by telling them, the lie will become the truth. For instance, you make fifty grand per, even though you know that you're really worth a lot more—say a hundred grand. And when somebody asks what you make, you ignore the fundamental impoliteness of the question and admit to making a hundred grand a year, since that comes a lot closer to the truth to which you aspire than the truth to which you must submit. The IRS really grooves on aspirational liars and gives them the greatest respect and understanding.

- *Lies of sales and seduction.* Salespeople often find that they have unwittingly told a lie by simply casting the truth in the most promising light. This does not alarm them. Here's how it goes: A woman asks you if you're married. You say, "Married? You know, I think it's sad how little commitment means to people these days. I think commitment is crucial to a society's health and sanity. How can we expect strangers to respect us if they have no respect for those they say they love?" Then you ask her if *she's* married, and the next thing you know, you're lying to your wife's lawyer.

Besides, you know you're on the wrong side of the moral tracks, even before you tell a lie. For instance, your wife asks a simple question: "Where have you been?" If you were at the hardware store, you don't even see the possibility of a saving falsehood. On the other hand, you don't have to wait to hear your gaseous attempt at self-exoneration to know the misdeed you committed down at Motel Six is going to look mighty ugly under the clear light of truth, which has, alas, been left on for you.

What to Do When the Waiter Comes Back to the Table and Says, "Sorry, Your Card's Been Denied"

This is a telling example of the **Main Thing** about etiquette:

The rules of etiquette exist not to make boors out of those who don't know them, but to make sure everybody feels as comfortable as possible in as many situations as possible.

- *Consider the comfort of your dinner partner.* Don't make the credit card problem a big deal, because it isn't one. It's nothing personal between you and the waiter, and it's nothing you can rectify on the spot. Don't feign outrage and indignation, and don't abuse the messenger. Simply acknowledge what has happened as an awkward situation—you're apparently over the limit imposed by the credit card issuer—and ask the waiter for a suggestion about other means of satisfying the bill, say, paying by personal check or with a charge card (which, unlike a credit card, has no fixed limit).

- *Consider the comfort of your waiter.* If none of the above means of payment is acceptable and you volunteer to run around the corner to an ATM for cash, it is proper manners to leave something behind of obvious value—your driver's license, for example, or your dinner companion.

- *Make a stink with your banker.* Having said the above, we should also say that it's awfully bad manners to impose a limit on a chap's credit, since it presumes his inability or unwillingness to repay the debt. This is a personal insult, of course, and one you may wish to bring up later, when you call the bank.

How to Make a Corncob Pipe

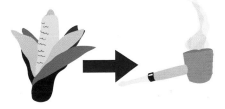

- ***Eat your corn.*** Butter up a nice ear of corn, one at least two inches thick. Yellow corn works better than white. Maize—or field corn—works pretty well, too, but you're talking cow chow here, so stick with what you can eat yourself.

- ***Dry your cob.*** You can do this either by letting it sit in a sunny window for a week or by drying it in a 150-degree oven for ten or twelve hours.

- ***Cut a cross section*** of the cob about two inches long for the bowl. Don't get ambitious: A three-inch bowl will be impossible to draw.

- ***Hollow it out*** with a pocketknife. If you're a good whittler, and you have a sharp knife (see the section "How to Keep Your Edge" in chapter 15), you can score the bowl around the top and just dig in. An alternative is to use a hole drill, then scoop out the center. Make sure to leave a wall of at least a half inch at the bottom—you don't want a lap full of hot ashes—and a quarter inch on the sides.

- ***Drill a hole*** in the side of the cob about a quarter inch above the insibe bottom of the cob.

- ***File it.*** You want to make the outside of the bowl smooth. Then apply a coat of shellac. Be careful not to shellac the top or inside, though.

- ***Use a short piece of bamboo*** and the plastic stem from another pipe to make the mouthpiece. Taper the end of the bamboo to make it fit inside the cob tightly. Secure the stem with epoxy or Krazy Glue. Fit the plastic pipe stem over the bamboo.

- ***Break it in.*** Fill the bowl of the pipe a little at first, then more with each sub sequent bowlful. Until the bowl is well seasoned, don't smoke the pipe hot.

- ***Find a porch.*** And while you're at it, find a rocker.

6. Women

We admit women are smarter than men, cuter than men, and more sensitive than men. In fact, we admit that women are superior beings in every way. There's only one thing we really want to know:

How to Become a Sex Object

You'd think, after all the careful scrutiny we have given to sex objects, we'd have a better idea how to be one ourselves, yes? No. Men are so convinced that they ought to be the sex subject of a sex object that they never give women a chance to objectify them. Alas, objectification is what separates friends from lovers.

Besides, sometimes our goals are not so lofty. Sometimes, all we want is to drive women insane with desire. Is that so much to ask? Not at all, not at all. The trick is to make the woman you love stop seeing you as a thinking, feeling, complex person with hopes and dreams and fears, and start seeing you as a sex object, a simple tool for doing a simple job.

Becoming a sex object is something within the grasp of Everyman. Here are five paths to objectification—along with more than a dozen object lessons—all of which will help you help others.

Caution: Each path is paved in peril. This is one more time when the end doesn't necessarily justify the means.

- **Path 1: The Path of Least Insistence**
- **Path 2: The Path of Most Insistence**
- **Path 3: The Path of Coexistence**
- **Path 4: The Path of Charitable Assistance**
- **Path 5: The Aisle**

Five paths, one goal: To get what you want out of a bedroom, other than a good night's sleep. Now, that's an object worth striving for.

FIRST PATH: DON'T TRY SO HARD

According to modern psychologists, men are motivated strongly by two easy-to-confuse commodities: money and sex. It's easy to see how an average man can mix these up. Money, after all, has a wonderful look and feel all its own. It's great to get a lot of money whenever you want, plus no matter how much you have or how often you get it, somebody else's money always looks better than yours. Also, you fool around with too much of it, you could get in trouble. You don't know where it's been.

While sex shares most of these qualities, most men find it easy to tell sex from money because it's often easier to get rich than it is to get laid. The reason for this is simple, but exquisitely unjust. Most men have been taught, rightly, that if you work very hard to make money, you'll eventually get it. This lesson, unhappily, is nontransferable when applied to romance, for if you work very hard to get sex, you'll die a virgin.

Case Study: Mr. F

Take a friend of ours, Mr. F. F lives in a swank Southern metropolis. After fleeing California when a relationship turned unexpectedly serious, F drifted through a half-dozen Eastern cities, pausing once in New York where he enjoyed, he said, "a certain kind of relationship" with a beautiful artist in a car parked in an alley, and once in Baltimore, where he was found in a cocktail lounge unable to handle his alcohol because the two women between whom he was sandwiched wouldn't take his hands from their laps. When he arrived in Dixieville, he was, he said, "automatically given women when I crossed the city line." After a monumental swivefest, he finally had to take a breather because he clocked himself in the noggin on a side table while performing some libidinal legerdemain. "Now I'm thinking about buying a house," he said when he came to, "and filling it with a wife and kids." Alas, he added, "good women are too easy to find."

All women love Mr. F, and, as a consequence, Mr. F is having sex for all the rest of us. Why? F understands that women are immensely interested in men who are pleasant, charming, witty, and, above all, pleased to be in their company without any expectations. "I guess sex just never crosses my mind," F said. "But it's nice when it crosses theirs." By not making women into sex objects, F allows them the liberty of making him into one, and he hates to disappoint.

Lessons of the First Path

- *Love overpacks,* so courtship can come with a lot of extra baggage. You don't always have to do all the heavy lifting, however.
- In the cafeteria of love, *there is such a thing as a free lunch.*
- *You usually get more than you need* if you don't ask for anything at all.

The First Path Downside

Mr. F (the example used in our case study) is miserable because he's no closer to a stable relationship than he was the day he first said "Howdy" to his sex life.

"This makes a quarter century of living like this," says F. "Maybe it's time I grew up or something."

SECOND PATH: GIVE IT EVERYTHING YOU'VE GOT

There is another side to the argument presented by Mr. F (for those of you who have trod completely through the first path). It's the one that says, if it isn't worth begging for, it isn't worth having.

An explanation: In the rhetoric of professional sports, nothing quite says nothing like the pitcher or the quarterback who, when asked how he did what he did, says, "I just do my best, I give it all I got, I give it 100 percent, I'm just glad to be out there." That's understatement. What the fellow means is that he brings to his chore a focused wholeness of desire, a burning need to succeed, a gut-bottom, soul-selling, white-hot, do-or-die intensity to achieve, without which his life will cease to have meaning.

This can work. Sometimes women, like men, lead lives of homogenized predictability—stark, unadorned, unfurnished, one-bedroom existences that cry out for a little ornamentation. Suddenly, there's a voice in the hall, a knock at the door. She opens it, and it's a maniac interior decorator with DayGlo spray cans in each hand. Next thing you know, her life looks like a Jimi Hendrix poster.

Case Study: El Coyote

A man whom we shall call the Coyote is a master of blitzkrieg lovecraft. Every encounter with a woman has a tactical dimension, every handshake lingers a little too long, every first glance is just a tad overfilled with nuance. Coyote sees an attractive woman, and he immediately thinks, "Road Runner." All of a sudden, huge, cast-iron safes full of romance are tumbling out of the sky, there are explosives everywhere, and, without being asked to, he's running off the edge of cliffs into thin air. Sometimes, a woman, bored with too much primetime TV,

sees this sort of behavior, says, "What the hell?" and is swept up into a pyrotechnical scene in which she realizes she's done all the things she swore she'd never do, including that Polaroid thing. So two weeks, two months later, she's saying, "Beep, beep," and vanishing into the landscape in a cloud of dust.

Mr. Coyote has winter wives and summer brides, but no relationship that stretches across more than two major holidays, for nothing can stand up to such an acute level of stress. That's why ball games last only nine innings. When it's over, it's over. But until then, the Coyote is 100 percent sex object and just glad to be out there.

Lessons of the Second Path

There are some things to be learned here, by the rocket's red glare:

- *If you're going to be a grizzly, be a bear.* There's no sense hoping some woman is going to grab you by the lapels of your sensitivity suit and rip your clothes off. Go naked.
- *Get rhythm.* If you want a romance to hip-hop, don't beat out a waltz.
- *Never sprint* if you're running a marathon.

The Second Path Downside

When it's over, it's over. But the problem, says the Coyote (of our case study), is that "every relationship I have is over, even before it's over, if you know what I mean."

Unfortunately, we know.

THIRD PATH: IF YOU CAN'T LICK 'EM, JOIN 'EM

We're surrounded by women, just "eat up in girls," as one writer put it. Their very ubiquity creates a certain demographic twist, in that most of the time, half the people we're with are the very people who can cause us greatest joy and profound anguish. It's the joy part you want.

So get to know them. Despite media-driven drivel, many women don't respond to overt empathy. In the real world, women and men like their partners to conform to comfortable stereotypes. But there are still plenty of women out there who are attracted to *hombres con mucho sensitivismo,* or weeping men who read their souls.

Case Study: Mr. Bill

Take, for our case study example, a chap of recent acquaintance whom we shall call Mr. Bill.

Mr. Bill isn't the most handsome guy, and while he can outwit his dinner, he's not a genius by any stretch. As a teenager, he was foiled in romance, just like the rest of us. Couldn't get to first base. But, in college in the 1960s, he learned that women, as dates, liked men who liked Women, as a movement. So he would take his dates to Germaine Greer lectures and feminist rallies. With the warm, cozy fires of the sexual revolution crackling in the background, he'd seek to raise the consciousness of his women friends, and when he heard women talking about how deeply moved they'd been by other women, he would feel the big wave of empathy smack him in the chops, and he'd weep, right out loud.

Women dug it. Mr. Bill was suddenly surrounded with women. Some of them looked a little on the earnest side, but some were pretty good looking, and some of them were also smarter than him—and capable of earning lots more money than he could—so he married one of those.

Mr. Bill is now a well-known man, and some women—total strangers, mind you—dream about him, nasty stuff, too. To them, he is a dreamboat, a sex object.

Lessons of the Third Path

- *Do whatever it takes,* so long as it's worth whatever you get.
- *Women who get serious* about sexual politics can also get serious about sex.
- *Even apparently humorless women* can take a joke for better or worse, for richer or poorer.

The Third Path Downside

You marry the woman, you marry the politics. When a third-path woman yells, "NOW!" you have to check whether she means the movement or the motion.

FOURTH PATH: LET WOMEN MAKE YOU A MAN

Men are often at odds with each other. Contentious from birth, men strive to vanquish one another, or, failing that, to find a quiet corner where other men will leave them alone. In commerce, this sort of thing is essential, since the game has been structured to be won, not to be tied. But in terms of the inner guy, where hope, self-esteem, and doubt all live in a troubled neighborhood, men wrestle with themselves, and women are the referees, the ones who decide who's a winner and who's a loser.

Case Study: Q

Take, for instance, a stockbroker whom we'll call Q, because of his extraordinary skill at snooker, billiards, and pool. Q lived a life of limitless success, moneywise. Q had the helium touch: He was apparently forbidden by fate from choosing a stock that was capable of downward movement. He was also a reasonably handsome man. Yet, he was filled with doubts. He would ask his friends hideous questions: "Do I seem stupid?" or "What can I talk about to make me seem important?" His friends were mortified for him, and so, of course, were the women he dated, since he sought from them some creepy affirmation, and they were the one place where it wasn't available.

One day, he met a woman whom he thought unattainable. His friends agreed, since she was obviously smart and confident and scenic. Remarkably, and to the immense confusion of his friends, the beauty liked Q. Was it the money? We'll never know, for eventually, they married, and Q settled down with his wife and his new, confident, interesting, concerned self. His friends watched this transformation in fear, but the marriage was apparently sound. Eventually, several of Q's friends pinned him in the pinball corner of a barroom and asked him how he had done it. "I didn't," Q said. "She did. She would pick a fight with me whenever I asked those stupid questions, the ones that made me look so lame. The fight would be about something else, something that didn't have anything to do with my doubts. Then she'd let me win the argument."

Q's wife refused to let him slip into full-nelson dorkness. In his new, more masculine wardrobe, he's her sex object.

Lessons of the Fourth Path

- *Women's work:* Some women know that if they want a man made right, they'd better make him themselves.
- *It's one thing to be a man among men.* It's another to be a man among women.
- *Mojo is like money.* If you have to ask whether or not you've got mojo, you haven't got it.

The Fourth Path Downside

What a good woman builds, an angry woman can tear down. If you want to make yourself a man, make it a do-it-yourself project.

FIFTH PATH: COMMIT TO IT

For many women—especially the ones you'd most like to have treat you as a sex object—nothing greases the slip 'n slide into the bedroom quite like a well-planned marriage ceremony. There's something in the cake that just makes a woman downright agreeable. If you need a case study to illuminate this timeless truth, your problems are bigger than any solution you'll find on the Web.

Not only that, but *the lessons of the Fifth Path* won't quite fit a list. They just show up every now and then over the course of a lifetime. One small lesson does recur, however: You may think you're strolling down paths one, two, three, or four, only to turn a corner and find yourself on five. Incredible.

The Downside

There's as much downside as you can fit in a lawyer's office. That's the bad news. But the good news is that there's always more upside than there is downside—even if you have to live through a pile of downside to get up.

You can reduce the downside of the Fifth Path by following simple numbers:

- *Fifty percent.* Cohabitation before marriage increases the chances of divorce by as much as 50 percent.
- *Eight years.* If you marry somebody, close your eyes, shut your mouth, and hang around for eight years. Statistically, marriages that last eight years have a terrific chance of lasting a lifetime.
- *One kid* is all it takes to make a couple into a family, and marriages with children have a higher success rate than childless marriages.

How to Tell If a Woman Likes You

Women's feelings of attraction to men are a little like the centrifugal clutch on a Subaru Justy: They start out just fast enough to get you going, catch up with you halfway down the stretch, and don't really hit top end until you're ready to stop. That means a woman's feelings toward you are manifested differently, according to where you are in the relationship.

- *It's a very straightforward deal:* She's attracted to you if she's still talking to you even though she doesn't have to. There are other symptoms of positive feminine response: Laughing at your lame jokes, touching your arm or leg when she talks to you, asking you about your incredibly dull job down at the gas works. We discuss at length, immediately below, the intrinsic meaning of extended, direct eye contact. If she does any of these things, you can safely ask her out for a first date.

- *Postdate reevaluation:* After you take her home, you have to reevaluate the deal. If you want to spend another four hours with her, and you think she wants to do the same with you, then call her up. You can figure a woman's attracted to you if she says she'd like to put herself through the whole thing again and go out to dinner next Saturday.

Bear in mind, however: **This is the start of a trajectory toward nudity that may or may not be interrupted by a marriage ceremony.** The whole course of a courtship is a constant escalation of mutual superficial attraction. We say "superficial" because you never really know whether or not a woman's feelings toward you are situational and subject to change without notice. In order to tell if a woman's really attracted to you, wait until she has your second child. Then you can figure you've got her attention for good, more or less.

THE RULE OF DOUBLE EYE CONTACT ON A SINGLE OGLE

Sometimes, trying to figure a woman's unstated intention can require a bit more deliberate analysis. For example: What does it mean when you're ogling a woman and she catches you at it and instead of looking away, returns a direct stare, not once, but *twice*?

- *The elements* of this case are simple:
  Two guys.
  A mall.
  An escalator.

Two women.
One ogle.
Two eye contacts.

- **The details:** A sunny day, but brisk. Two friends decide to meet for lunch at a downtown enclosed shopping mall. There's a quick dash into a Brooks Brothers outlet, where a suit is purchased within three minutes. Then there's lunch.

The dining area at the mall is one of those American adaptations of a Euro-trough, the standard street café, where people sit and look at other people until they are caught, at which time they stare intently at their corned beef sandwiches. Next to the café is an escalator, and next to the descending half of the escalator is where our two chaps encamp for a quick bite. One guy is married, and he has his back to the escalator. He can't see anything, girl-wise. The other guy is single, and he can see everything. The escalator practically dumps shoppers at his feet.

The conversation is a heavily fragmented one. The married man, his back to the scenery, is talking about media coverage of the deficit. The single guy is frequently distracted by the sudden appearance and descent of one or another metropolitan beauty. In the middle of a sentence, typically, the bachelor clams up, raises one eyebrow in a sullen smolder, and, frankly, *ogles.* He's been doing this for years, of course, and his scan is a well-practiced one. As a face man, he starts there. The face is his screening device. Bad face, back to the deficit. Good face, go directly to the shoes. He ogles like a bibliophile, like a man who knows exactly which details and nuances create desirability, and which ones are fatal flaws. The married guy waits patiently for the appraisal.

- **Let's digress for a moment to consider the narcissistic corollary:** Men ogle not to fantasize about women, but to see how they measure up as men.

The mall ogler's pastime is not a gender-specific one, of course. Women ogle as much as the next guy. Usually, they ogle other women, although since their mission in ogling is essentially fact gathering—why did she wear that scarf? you call that eyeshadow? nice pumps—it may be demeaning to ogling to call it ogling. Women sometimes ogle men. That's ogling. Ogling is when you look at somebody in an effort not so much to evaluate the person being ogled, but to evaluate your own ogling self. For example, a man looks at a woman crossing the street. He ogles her. Generally—and there are certainly exceptions to this corollary—he is making a precise calculation that involves this equation: Beauty plus availability divided by self-image equals relative worth of ogler. There are many tiny variables that can nudge the ultimate solution one way or another. For instance, you might look at a beautiful passerby and find she is almost certainly out of range of your ability to attract women. Maybe the self-image part of the equation is just too low, or her beauty + availability number is just too high. But then you say to yourself, "Sure, that's now. But with a dash of Rogaine, a few years on Somali-Fast, and a Samsonite full of C-notes, she'd be at my feet." Suddenly, your projected self-image numbers rise, and you find it more and more likely not only that she could be yours (if you really wanted) but that maybe you wouldn't have time for her, what with all the other women around.

But back to the double eye contact on a single ogle rule. When a normal guy is ogling, part of what he's actually doing is just thinking about what politely might be called a relationship. But sometimes in ogling, as in all relationships, things sort of sneak up on you. After a burger-and-fries worth of idle ogling, the single guy suddenly pales. "I got eye contact," he says tensely, almost grimly. "No, wait. That's it." His voice drops to a burdened whisper. "I got *double* eye contact."

Significance of Double Eye Contact on a Single Ogle

- *This response is a gesture of commitment* more meaningful than many marriages. When a woman returns an ogle with a mere single glance, it can mean anything. Might mean: What's-he-staring-at-is-there-toilet-paper-on-my-shoe? Might mean: Let's-see-what-kind-of-jerk-I'm-dredging-off-the-bottom-of-the-gene-pool-today. Might mean: Make-a-move-and-I-call-the-cops. Hence, most men disregard the single glance to an ogle response. Single glances used to mean something. But with the widespread availability of go-go dancers, all of whom are quite accomplished in the art of making prolonged single-gesture eye contacts with oglers in bulk, a glance doesn't carry much weight anymore. A double glance in response to an ogle, however, is something else. Double eye contact on a single ogle means this: I know you're watching me, and I think you're sort of marginally interesting, and I think I'll see what you're made of, buster.

So. You ogle. She does a double take. Now what do you do? If you look away, too stunned or embarrassed to continue ogling, you're scrapple. A guy too cowardly to stand up for his own ogle isn't much of a man in most women's books. But if you continue to ogle in the face of a double glance, the ball's back in her court. If she looks away, no point. If she smiles, you can figure you've been asked to politely identify yourself, your motives, your marital standing. If your papers are in order, you get permission to cross the line, to go the next step. Whatever that is.

OTHER OGLING SCENARIOS
The Never-Fail Principle of Bad Timing

- *Women almost never return an ogle until your wife or girlfriend is looking*—first at the woman, wondering who she's smiling at, then at you, when she figures it out.

- Because men ogle as a means of taking stock of themselves, they know *there's nothing intrinsically threatening* to the whole activity. Men don't ogle, after all, because they want to. They ogle because they have to. It's horrible. Call it ogle burden. It's what we do, and sometimes a man's gotta do what a man's gotta do.

That's why different men ogle in different ways. Involved men out with the objects of their involvement do an indirect ogle. They look around the supermarket as if they'd never seen anything quite like it before. Look at those lighting fixtures! they seem to be saying. And how about those metal shelving units! Their necks are suddenly rubberized for such occasions, and the fact that a clearly ogleable woman just happens to be in their line of sight is pure coincidence. That way, if the woman responds to the ogle with a smile, the guy can always look at his ferocious wife and shrug. Men know they can ogle their brains out and never get so much as a notice until one fine, spring day when an ogling kind of guy and his principal sugar-pie are out for a stroll. He tosses off an inconsequential ogle and presto! He gets a double—no! a triple—take in return. Then he starts explaining.

Competitive Ogling by Guys in Packs

A woman walks down the street, and there's a wild pack of oglers staring at her. She nervously glances over to make sure they aren't armed oglers, and instantly every man claims eye contact. "She was looking at me, man," one of them says, while the others produce documentary evidence refuting the claim.

- *A single-man ogle is a serious thing.* Women know that. That's why they never seem to respond.

The Law of the Knowing Glance

- *Here, the situation is reversed:* The woman is the ogler, and you are the oglee. There are two basic ways of handling this. One involves ignoring the ogle, a decision made after the all-important first glance. She ogles. You glance. In a nanosecond, you have to process a great deal of information, all of it effervescently superficial and exactly the kind of information on which men make all important decisions, like whether or not to look again.
- *If you take the second look,* you might be well-advised to invoke the law of the knowing glance, which says an ogle is always trumped by a leer. In other words, you slowly look up and meet her gaze, while on your face you wear an expression that says, "Was that good for you?"

This has the effect of ram-injecting the encounter and giving it a NASA-level rate of acceleration. Suddenly, you're not just two strangers exchanging a goggles for gapes. You're on intimate terms, and with you, Mr. Mojo, in the driver's seat. You saw her ogle and raised her an innuendo. You can't lose. If she looks away, give her five minutes, and she'll ogle again. If she smiles, you can figure your glance was good enough that you can roll over and go to sleep. Either way, you'll have this encounter in the bag, if you'll pardon the play on words.

The Obviated Ogle Injunction

- *An ogle is diminished by overshadowing eccentricities.*

Let's say you're sitting alone in a subway car when a gaggle of art school painters' models—women who have been ogled with aesthetic passion—gets in. They're young, they're beautiful, and they stare right at you. But you're wearing a Santa suit and darning your socks. All ogles are off. No return glances are scored, and your self-image numbers are expressed in negatives.

How to Make Small Talk with Your Server

Speaking of direct eye contact, one nice thing about waitresses is they all look right at you, at least once. And when a great-looking woman comes at you with a handsome pile of food in each hand, you're forgiven for thinking you're as close to the goddess as you're ever likely to be: You're looking at man's version of protowoman, Eve with a side order of apple, Salome with that head, Mom with lunch.

After all, a wide variety of men may admire a wide variety of women for a wide variety of reasons. But all us fellers agree that *no other combination of primary elements so clearly comes close to the gratification of every man's principal desires as a beautiful woman bearing food.* For the ugly truth is, we're hounds for chow and slaves for sex, and we can skip the brains and soul part if we really, *really* have to, no sweat. In fact, it is in our early, formative encounters with waitresses that we first confuse nature and nurture—men who were breastfed as babies, for instance, almost always marry waitresses—and after that, it takes a lifetime of lunches to get it all straight.

WHAT WE SEE WHEN WE SEE A WAITRESS

On one level, of course, we see future bank vice presidents and tele-journalists, embalmers and actresses. We see hardworking moth-ers with kids and patient ex-wives with deadbeat ex-husbands. We see nurses without needles and divorcees without lawyers. But on another, shamefully intuitive level, we also see **temporary wives who make perfect flapjacks,** serve 'em up hot and with a spicy little quip, then get out of the way. All across this great land of ours, men are wolfing down hash like so many turbaned pashas, surrounded by a seraglio of women who allow sports pages on the table and don't go on about the dishes.

But remember, *inside every waitress is a woman who wants very much to be served.* This unfulfilled dream accounts for almost every surly waitress on the planet, because instead of men in waiters' suits bustling around with bottles of expensive bubbly, there's a counter-full of joes like you and me, and we quite obviously don't know how to behave.

HOW TO MAKE THE WAITRESS'S WORLD
A BETTER PLACE

Waitresses ask so little—just three small things, really:

- *Whatever it is you were going to say, don't, because she's already heard it a million times.* In the course of a forty-hour week, a good-looking waitress hears every conceivable variation on the are-you-on-the-menu-sweetheart? theme. The sad fact: Waitresses generally only talk to men because if they didn't they'd get the order wrong.

- *Don't confuse food with favors.* In the feverish first blush of satia-tion, men sometimes confuse the message with the messenger and think that because the turkey's mighty friendly to an empty stom-ach, the turkey toter will give a similar satisfaction. In reality, of course, waitresses don't care how hungry you are. Waitresses are simply paid members of the serving profession—which is a long rung above the caring professions. Members of the clergy *care.* Social workers *care.* Waitresses *serve.* When it comes to animal desires, most men prize good service above genuine concern. When a man is hungry, he wants pot roast, not a sympathetic analysis of the root causes of his condition.

- *Always overtip.* Think about what a waitress goes through. Every embarrassment our gender can muster is displayed before a waitress at work, where the daily special's an all-you-can-take bad manners buffet. For minimum wage, she has to put up with you and cousin Larry, the guy who *always* asks a waitress what kind of pie she has. For her, life at work is like being a professional pedestrian working a construction site. Why is she wearing that tight, white, little, semitransparent dress? Because she wants us to admire her incredible body and applaud her good taste in lingerie? Yeah, sure, maybe. But maybe she wears that dress because the owner, a guy named Nick, told her she has to.

All this—for minimum wage, no benefits.

Her side of this stupendous deal requires her to act in good faith toward all comers, to treat all men as though they were gentlemen, and to chuckle indulgently when they aren't. Plus, she's expected to be nice when some putz rounds *down* to a ten percent tip.

A FINAL NOTE CONCERNING WAITRESS-COURTSHIP

Every waitress's dream date involves food served by someone other than herself. Follow the rules in the next section.

How to Pitch Woo

Valentine's Day comes only once a year, but the aftershock of forgetting it can shake a romance all year long. So do it right.

- *Femme faves:* Romantic dinners, two dozen roses (one in the morning, one at night), a pro massage, a diamond engagement ring, a puppy, a weekend escape to a surprise-and-no-tell destination.
- *What to skip:* Chocolates, sappy cards, books of sappy poems, vinyl nighties, drinks at Club Les Gals, you in a loincloth.

How to Avoid Marriage

If staying single is what you consider to be a worthwhile goal, here're the best ways to ensure you'll be successful:

- ***Be especially careful*** between now and your twenty-ninth birthday. By then, half of all men have been married at least once.
- ***Don't get too lax*** after your twenty-ninth birthday, either. Or at least contain yourself until you turn thirty-five. At that point, if you have never been married, the odds are ten to one that you never will be.
- ***Until you turn thirty-five,*** you might consider spending all of your free time in bars and clubs, since almost no one ever meets a prospective mate in places like that.
- ***Places to avoid:*** schools, churches, and offices. In organizations specializing in social services and physical therapy, women outnumber men two to one.

How to Say Sayonara

There are few moments as illuminating as the moment you first realize that not only are you not with the one you love, you can't even love the one you're with. This split second of clarity comes with the intensity of a welder's arc. Most men simply look away for a second, then open their eyes again when the moment passes.

But what do you do when the light's always in your eyes? What do you do when your leg is in the trap and the only way you can see getting out is to gnaw it off at the knee? What do you do when you're the one who realizes the household stench is from rotting love? How do you get out and let a little air in?

- ***Here's the situation:*** You meet a woman, you fall in love. Then it's love, love, love for a few months. Then it's not. Suddenly, you're the impacted molar in the jaw of romance, and you face, head-on, the gruesome realization that the extraction of a man from love gone bad is long, painful, and leaves behind a remorseless throb. What's a man to do? You know you have to end it, but how? How

do you tell somebody you were just kidding about that love thing? How do you get out of a relationship that has you in the genital compactor? How, after all that time and effort spent getting in, are you going to get out?

- *We have the answers,* assuming you have the right problem. Here's what works for those involved in a less-than-marital kind of hogpen. However, please note: If your problem also involves something like a wedding vow, you might need to do a little more research.

TWO WAYS TO LEAVE YOUR LOVER

Basically, and Paul Simon's advice notwithstanding, *there are only two ways to leave your lover:* There's the easy way, and there's the hard way

Slip out the back, Jack

The easy way seems so easy it's hard to imagine why anybody would do it the hard way. Think of the relationship as a machine with only one moving part—you. One day you're there, the next day you're not, like the guy who says to his wife and five kids, "Hey, everybody, I'll be right back, just going out for a newspaper," and the next thing they know, he's living in Seattle with a cocktail waitress he met at a bowling alley in Tucson.

In every logical way, this is how love should end: "I'll be right back," then you're gone. No fuss, no muss, no crying and carrying on.

Is there a catch? You bet. Several, in fact:

- *You have to hear the fat lady sing.* Resolution counts, especially in a complex relationship. She'll want the whole thing resolved right away so she can get on with her life. You won't want to give her that, naturally, because it will be uncomfortable for you. But someplace down the line, you may want a little resolution, too—especially if this sort of exit turns into a routine. Lonely guys sometimes wonder how they ever got so lonely. Their ex-girlfriends could tell them, no problem.

- *You have to pay your debts.* If some woman is willing put up with the incredibleness of you, you owe her the dignity of making a decorous exit—and you owe it to yourself to make the last gesture of the relationship the one that invests the romance with a little meaning. Why? Charity aside, you have to remember that it's not just her relationship that's ending, it's yours, too. You invested your share of time and trauma.

- *You might want to look back.* It's one thing to burn a bridge. It's quite another to blow up the dam, too. Slipping out the back leaves such an indelible stain of resentment behind that if you ever want to pass that way again, it'll be impossible. Not only will she detest you forever, but so will her family and friends, and so will some of yours, since few men admire men who have no honor.

- *It's unrealistic.* This is the real reason you can't just steal away in the night: People are too complicated for that sort of thing. There will be things you want to say that she won't want to hear, and things she'll say you won't like much, either. As a rule, people never simply walk away from affairs unless they never took the affairs seriously to begin with.

The Hard Way

Before you say anything, before you shut the door forever, sit still a minute and *think about what's happening.* Most men, when it comes to break-up time, are looking only about ten minutes down the road. They see the front door and the bright light outside. They see the big so-long, then they see a five-hundred-yard straightaway. But there are curves in that road, and one of them might be just sharp enough to throw you into the ditch of despair.

- *Count your losses.* When you say "adios," it'll be the last rational word you'll speak or hear. Know where you're going once you leave. Figure out if what you're going to get is better or just different. Do a quality check on your present household model: Trustworthy? Loyal? Helpful? Courteous? Kind? Obedient? Cheerful? Thrifty? Clean? Reverent? Good-looking when naked? One guy, a Pennsylvania-based pilot, abruptly left a woman he'd been with for four years to go to another woman who threw him out after two weeks. His analysis: "Bad move."

- *You or her?* Be honest with your own self-serving self for a sec. Which one of you two has the problems in this deal?

Here's one way to find out: Tell yourself the story of your relationship as if it were a movie. Okay, okay, not a great movie, maybe, but a movie nonetheless. Who's the hero? Who's the villain? Once you have your tale down pat, run it past a good friend. Let him ask questions. Let him decide who the villain is. Don't be alarmed if a relatively objective rewrite gives your little drama a surprise ending.

If it's her, no sweat. You get the moral edge and she gets a free education.

If it's you, you get to do this over and over again until you figure out how to put the blame where it belongs.

EXTRACTION STRATEGIES

Once you figure out exactly what's wrong, you've got to do the heavy lifting required to get yourself out of that quagmire you're in. Here are some field-tested romance breakers.

Make a Fight

Pick a fight, make it a whopper, get plenty of yelling and screaming going, say what you want, do what you want short of violence, but just make sure it's about the Big Issue—the one thing that really is your last straw. This can be anything from squeezing the toothpaste tube the wrong way to squeezing the postman the right way, but keep your main peeve in the foreground. "The thing that cracked it for me was how she'd blow up whenever we fought," said Tim, a Pittsburgh artist. "Didn't matter what it was about, she'd start throwing things— bottles, food, anything. Once, she threw a hammer at me. So I said I was fed up with that crap, I was leaving ... then, she really went ballistic."

Upside: Not only will you have spelled out your grievance clearly, you'll also have enough anger built up to actually carry you out the door. "I had to leave, or die."

Downside: Screaming out loud is usually a poor way to engage in analytical discourse. "She called three days later," Tim recalled, "and said she couldn't remember what we had been fighting about. Is that crazy crap or what?"

Make a Mess

One surefire way to spell breakup is to have your honey walk into the bedroom while you're lying in bed sandwiched between two steaming Samoan stewardesses. Gene, a hotel worker from Las Vegas, said that one of the reasons he moved to Nevada was the "extremely high numbers of women between the ages of twenty-eight and thirty-four who are great looking, employed, and single." Gene says he makes his segues "extremely seamlessly, where I just get the next woman to move in before the last one moves out. This," he adds gravely, "always seems to work."

Upside: Gene's right. It works.

Downside: The $625,000 lawsuit Gene got hit with last August from his last girlfriend came on the heels of a previous settlement that cost him his house. "She owns the place now," he said. Gene was toying

with an idea recently about rekindling his romance with the new owner of his house, "but she's still pissed." Some women are never happy.

Make a Stand

Compose a statement of belief, something comprehensive, clean, forthright, and unambiguous. Think it through carefully and thoroughly. Couch it in the terms normally used to express deeply held convictions: "I cannot respect someone who eats kippered herring in bed." Clearly spell out the reasons you have for wanting to call it quits, and try to keep your emotions in check while you do it. Be compassionate and considerate, but not patronizing. Leave no question unanswered, and make certain you are on firm moral ground by tying everything to an ethical point of view. Allow for a certain amount of vituperation, and offer to continue the conversation later if she becomes airborne. Show no anger. Mention love; use words like "care" and "profound." Never allow a hint of ambivalence.

Upside: You will have given her the chance to keep her dignity by guarding your own.

Downside: Disappointment. It must be noted that this approach is nearly impossible. As a rule, it's the way most men start out, but they get distracted by shouts, screams, knives, something that changes the direction or the tenor of the conversation. "I tried to tell her sort of politely," said Tim, "but she just wouldn't have it that way." There are no soft spurns, apparently.

Make a Deal

This strategy is one tailor-made for the man who wants out of the relationship he's in and wants to build a new relationship—but with the same woman. Here's the angle: **Figure out what it is she is doing that you just can't stand.** Then tell her you might be back if she'll fix whatever it is that's broke. To use a real-life but awesomely downmarket example, let's say you're like Bill, a native of Nebraska, and the thing that is driving you away is her constant nagging about the dead fish you keep bringing in and tossing in the sink with the dishes. "That's just me," asserts Bill. "That's who I am. I love to fish, she doesn't—and she doesn't like anything about fishing, either." Trivial? Perhaps to you, and obviously unimportant to Bill's girlfriend. But not to Bill. Fishing, to

Bill, is like golf to aging yuppies, or like God to Baptists. "Fishing's the end-all, as far as I'm concerned. I don't need to do nothing else." Nor, presumably, anyone else, either. Anyway, let's say your beef is with the fish you catch and that she won't clean. That's the thing that's wrong. So you say, "What's so bad about cleaning a fish every now and then?" And she says, "They stink. You kill 'em, you clean 'em and get 'em off the Limoges." Now you lay out your nonnegotiable blueprint: You work out a recovery plan for her. You say, "Look, honey, it's a two-step thing: First, get your china out of the sink, and, second step, clean fish when I catch them, otherwise [as Bill put it] color me gone." She may decline, but at least you've established some means by which she can, if she so desires, retrieve you.

Upside: Humane, and holds out the possibility of redemption, always nice. After all, if she's willing to change whatever it is that's bothering you, assuming that's the real issue, how could you do better? In fact, like all these tactics we've listed here, this one simply involves isolating the problem, then deciding whether it can be solved. Some problems can't be. But for those that can, this strategy provides a means for the solution.

Downside: You might have to learn to clean fish.

SEX, SEDUCTION, AND RELATIONSHIP MANNERS

Why lump these three things together? Because this illustrates how two apparently rude and mannerless enterprises can eventually lead to a situation in which manners are everything. Goes to show that good etiquette resembles a food chain, in which swinging occupies the bottom link, and marriage occupies the top, and divorce lawyers represent rabid mutants with bolt cutters.

How to Work with Women Without Becoming Paranoid

What with the current political climate, lots of guys are worried about being sent up to the Big House for sexual harassment.

- ***Don't worry. Be happy. And be polite.*** Look, you can't run your life according to your fears. If you are cordial and friendly and— above all—polite to the women in your office, nobody's going to be able to nail you on a bum charge of sexual harassment. Obeying the rules of etiquette are critical here, since that's what will keep you on the good-guy side of a bad-guy-good-guy conflict. Not only that, but times are a-changin', at last, and the personnel police are catching on to the excesses at large in this area. Angry women with attitudes used to be able to destroy a man's career on a whim. No more. Now they need witnesses and proof of a pattern of bad behavior before they can send you packing. So demonstrate instead a pattern of mannerly behavior, and not only will you be safe and sound, you'll also be wildly popular among most women, who are suckers for a well-polished dude who can hold open the door and tip his hat on cue.

How to Meet a Beautiful Woman

The operative principle is that even though a woman is beautiful, she merits consideration as a human being. This platitude comes courtesy of a woman who is a looker and tells us that she is sick of men who assume the best way to make her acquaintance is to insult her. "Why," she asked, "can't men just say 'Hello'?"

The answer, of course, is that "Hello" has no hook. It's not what we call a sell line. And for men, seduction is nothing more than salesmanship with a higher-than-average commission at stake.

Therefore, the polite thing to do is remove all that goal-oriented effluvia from the implications of a simple introduction. The rules of an introduction are simple:

- *If a mutual friend is making the introductions, a man is always presented to a woman.* "Trixie? I'd like you to meet my buddy, Ralph, Ralph Cooper. Coop, Trixie Rockefeller."
- *If you're introducing yourself, mention your name before asking for hers.* "Hello, I'm Van. Van Boutons." Then make a subtle gesture as if to stick out your hand for a quick shake, but don't go through with it until she offers hers. The rules say that a man must wait until a woman first offers her hand for a handshake. Otherwise, no hands are shaken. A side benefit: By holding back in this way, you can avoid the embarrassment of standing there with an unshaken hand. If she doesn't reply with her own name,

you know two things: (1) she's rude, and (2) nothing, no matter how witty and inventive, will be sufficient to induce her into a conversation, since she's already completely aware that a casual conversation may well be the first step along a slippery slope that can ultimately lead to a situation such as that addressed in the following instruction.

What to Say If You Can't Quite Get It Up

- *Don't whine.* The rude response is to apologize abjectly and claim that you don't understand because it's never happened before, ever. This type of apology only makes her responsible for what is clearly your problem, and the lie serves only to suggest that your partner is so hideous that she takes the fairy dust right out of your wand.

- *Take it like a man.* The polite response is to express mild disappointment: "Gee, too bad." Then you can get on to other things, since flaccidity need not stand between you and your partner's pleasure.

How to Handle a Jealous Lover

- *If you weren't at Motel 6,* but really were out of gas on the interstate, then politely explain to your wife the rudeness of assuming infidelity. Jealousy is a fine and mannerly barometer of affection. But unrestrained suspicion is the symptom of a larger problem, and the best thing to do is stop what you're doing and get it straightened out. Don't neglect your own possible culpability, either. Is there something you're doing—or not doing—that might warrant her suspicions?

- *If you were at Motel 6,* no polite explanation will wash away the indelible rudeness of your behavior. You are then faced with two rude alternatives: Confess all. Or deny all. Either way, there's a real good chance you'll soon have an opportunity to discover the etiquette of alimony. Which brings us to:

How to Handle an Angry Ex-Lover

The final **Main Thing** in etiquette is this: In an embarrassing or awkward situation in which all other remedies have failed, do one thing: *Disappear.*

That doesn't mean you should move to Rio and change your name. It does mean you should forward your alimony or child support payments through the mail, and make any other contact as formal and brief as possible.

What you learn from all this is that it pays to learn marital manners on the honeymoon, and to never forget them. Why? Because divorce, as those who have been there already know, is the institutional, legal response to bad behavior, in which she was rude to you, and you to her, until you both needed lawyers to spell out all the rules of post-matrimonial etiquette. And that can be a rude awakening, indeed.

How to Lie

Here, check out this trusty, old, yellowed Bible, the one with the hole clear through it from the time it stopped an assassin's bullet. Thumb through its singed pages, still covered with ash from when it gave protection from the great fire. Someplace in the Book is a piece of suitable moral armor, just the right size for everybody: We call these the rules of the game, but theologians call them the Ten Commandments. Most of them contain pretty good advice—no fooling around with the matron next door, no cussing allowed, and please don't kill anybody. But what about this one: "Thou shalt not bear false witness against thy neighbor"?

This one, of course, may well be a lie. You *have* to bear a little false witness every now and then, or you're dead meat, socially speaking. The reason you know that is because you lie all the time. You gotta. After all, there are plenty of good reasons for bearing false witness, while there are only a few good reasons not to. Thus, this small lesson in what we must call Survival Lying.

How to Choose a Perfect Gift

There are two kinds of presents. One kind goes to all your buddies, your coworkers, your relatives. The other kind goes to your wife or girlfriend.

- **Type one:** The rule to giving a memorable gift is thoughtfulness. That ramshackle cliché requires explanation: Your gift has to suggest that you thought about it, not that you're actually a thoughtful person. So go for ambiguity: Skip the fruitcakes and soap collections, for instance, and pick up something at the local junk emporium or antique shop. Some  weird, old artifact—an ancient egg poacher, a deco toaster—will set you back a sawbuck tops, but it'll seem to say something more personal, something more meaningful, but nobody'll know exactly what.

- **Type two:** Your wife or girlfriend has already told you *exactly* what she wants. So don't try to outwit her by selecting something she hasn't even thought of. If she hasn't thought of it, she doesn't want it. Instead, take her suggestion, add some money to it and upgrade to the next-best model. Unless, that is, she's asked for a weekend in Mazatlán with you.

How to Make Business Trips with Women

Pack the right assumptions: Here are some observations on mobile manners you might want to take along next time you hit the road on business, coed-style.

- **It's just business, stupid.** It's not a date. When men and women travel on business together, you can avoid any discomfort or misunderstandings by assuming she will always pay her own way—in the same way that you would expect a man you were traveling with would. Let's face it, an expense account knows no gender.

- **_Professional protocol takes precedence._** Offering to pay all the time, as you would in a social situation, is wrong in the company's point of view—plus it puts you both in an awkward position professionally; it's awkward if she is your superior, because it transfers a form of control to you when you should be deferring all such control to her, and if you are her superior it creates a situation that, we're sorry to say, could lead her to feel that she "owes" you, and that, we're even sorrier to say, could lead to things like charges of sexual harassment. In other words, unless you have something in mind other than business, let her pay her own way.

- **_Polite porterage?_** Some guys say you should let her carry her own bags. If that represents progress for women, so be it. Maybe that's just the way things are nowadays. But there are obvious limits. If your hands are free, help her out. On the other hand, on a business trip, there is no reason for her to stand at the curb waiting as you make two or three trips with things piled up in your arms to load up the car. In that case, she should help you carry things.

  Three rules of thumb:

1. If something needs to be lifted that is heavy or large, you do it regardless of whose bag or parcel it is.

2. Take her cue. If she seems to be saying, "I'll do it and if you try to help me I'll give you a black eye," then by all means, let her tote it.

3. Let courtesy and common sense dictate what you do in any given situation.

- **_Be politely sociable._** When you are traveling with a woman on business, you should invite her along with you on recreational outings—golf, a workout in the hotel's gym, a run—just as you would invite another guy if you were traveling with him. You may well hope she won't join you, but you should invite her anyway to avoid an uncomfortable situation. _This is especially true when there are two men and a woman traveling together._ It would be very impolite for two men go off together and leave a woman behind, unless it was her choice to stay behind.

- **Be careful.** Romance is everywhere, like the common cold germ. When you travel on business with a woman, you have to remember a couple of things: First, you may have no interest in her romantically, but that doesn't mean she feels the same way. And second, if a misunderstanding arises and gets blown out of proportion, public sentiment and the law are on her side, and any accusation of sexual misconduct or harassment by her about you—true or not—will be taken as the gospel. Unlike any other aspect of legal life, accusations of sexual misconduct of any kind are sufficient to convict in the court that matters—your own life. By just being at the other end of a pointed finger, you can suffer severe consequences, including a ruined career and a broken marriage. In fact, any time you're alone with a woman coworker, no matter how well you know her, you need to think of your situation the same way a woman looks at walking down a dark, deserted street late at night: *You're at risk, and you'd better be able to protect yourself.*

When traveling with a woman, keep your wits about you. Although most women would never dream of making an unwarranted claim of sexual harassment, you don't really know if the one you're with is one of the few who would. The world's full of lunatics, and some of them are pretty good looking. Keeping your wits about you means controlling circumstances that can spiral out of control easily: For instance, when you have a meeting with a woman colleague in a hotel room, make sure you are appropriately dressed—and if she is not, do not enter until she is. Also, avoid booze; once you reach a certain point, it gets harder to gauge the impact of the things you say and how they will be taken.

How to Dance a Jig

Sure, and another St. Pat's Day office party, and there you are with a lampshade on your head and no way short of conversation to tell the world what a happy chappy you really are. The solution: our original, two-footed, one-man, completely obliterated Irish jig.

- ***Get off on the right foot:*** Start by hopping up on your left foot and bring your right foot over and in front of your left, so your right toe touches the floor just in front of your left foot.
- ***Then reverse the whole proposition:*** Left toe on the ground in front of your right foot.
- ***Then back where you started,*** with your right toe on the mat. Now the tricky part:
- ***Jump back, Jack:*** Jump backward three times, like a Bunny Hop in full-throttle reverse. Pick yourself up, man, and try again: This time, use both feet. Don't even try hopping backward with your ankles crossed, even when you're completely sober.
- ***Take it from the top:*** Start again, with the right toe in front of your left foot. That's all there is to it. To really dress up the performance, you can tie your suit coat around your waist like a wee kilt, put one hand on your hip and the other up in the air, and make a little Gaelic whoop from time to time. Fancy Irish guys wiggle their toes a little before they bring them down to the ground. You'll look like a drunk hailing a cab, of course, but, at some point in the evening, that's what this is all about, no?

7. The Great Outdoors

The world is crowded with living things. In some places, like China, most of them are human. But in most places, when you're talking about dominant life-forms, you're talking plants and animals. Plants first:

HOW TO GROW GRASS

Nothing's weirder than the suburban fascination with grass—a labor-intensive, capital-sucking, crazy crop with no known market or secondary use beyond some light mulching. Yet, when you buy into the American dream, you also get the American nightmare: Lawn Care.

The moral imperative: When you own a house with a yard and lawn, you are morally obligated to do three things with the grass:

1. Water it.
2. Fertilize it.
3. Mow it.

How to Water the Lawn

There are **four factors** to consider here:

1. *The type of grass* you have.
2. *The soil* in your yard.
3. *The weather* in your area.
4. *The location* of your lawn.

It's always better to water your lawn only when it absolutely needs it. Not only is overwatering wasteful, it also makes your lawn a target for disease. In addition, it makes the grass grow faster, and we all know what that means.

How to Mow the Lawn

The big trick here is how to tell the grass needs to be cut without waiting for your neighbors to say so.

- *The rule of a green thumb* for this is you should cut the grass when it's about a third taller than the height recommended for the species. If it grows too long and you cut it, you can actually shock the grass, because you'll expose parts of the blades that have never had any exposure to sunlight before, and, bang! the grass turns yellow. A consistent height for your grass is the best bet.

- *Forget raking up lawn cuttings.* Turns out that if you keep the height of your lawn at a fairly consistent level and let the short trimmings land where they do, they will decompose and help your lawn stay healthy by providing it with lots of nutrients. However, if you cut your lawn after it has grown real long, you'll

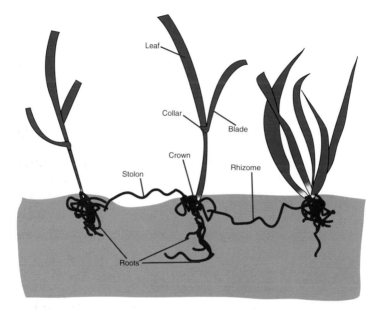

pile a thatch on top of your lawn and prevent the grass from getting the sunlight and air it needs, and, bang! the grass turns yellow.

HOW TO MOW THE LAWN REAL FAST

It can take several hours to mow a one-acre lawn on a typical riding mower. This isn't surprising, since the average mower has a top-end of five or six miles per hour, and an average cutting speed of only two or three miles per hour. How to speed up the process? Follow these simple instructions to boost your *cutting* speed up to an excellent forty-five miles per hour.

- ***Change the gear ratio.*** The first thing you have to do to get a higher speed is to change the gear ratio. Most machines have a three-inch pulley on the engine, and they run between a ten- or twelve-inch pulley in the back. Change the pulleys so you can put more revolutions per minute on the transmission. That means, of course, that you also have to:

- **Change the transmission.** Replace the stock tranny found on most lawn mowers with a right-angle gearbox. That allows you to have a gear ratio of 1:1.

- **Mount low friction bearings** in the back of the chassis and use a solid shaft for an axle. Mount a sprocket on the axle and a sprocket on the output of the right-angle gearbox. This allows you to set up a disk brake.

- **Reinforce the machine.** Stock chassis are made out of sheet metal. When you want to torture your machine, you have to put in some struts. While you're at it, replace all the bushings with bearings.

- **Lower the machine** a little bit to get a lower center of gravity. You can do this by altering the front axle to drop the front suspension as much as six inches. You can also install smaller tires. This will help with cornering, preventing little tufts of grass from surviving your passing blades.

If you want to get into some organized lawn mower racing, call the United States Lawn Mower Racing Association at (708) 729-7363.

HOW S**T HAPPENS

Attention, happy composters: If you are into recycling at all, somewhere near you someone is throwing away tons of stuff that the plants in your yard and house would like to have as food. All you have to do is go get it or tip the guy who brings it to you for free.

We're talking organic waste here, from cow and chicken manure to decomposing fish to tons and tons of apple and blueberry waste. It's the smelly stuff that will make your garden grow. Here's how to get it:

First find your favorite waste. Almost anything that comes from the earth can be composted and returned to the earth as fertilizer. Someplace near you, somebody is making money from cows, chickens, horses, fish, seaweed, shellfish, cotton, carrots, celery, lettuce, tomatoes, potatoes, whey, hops, berries, mushrooms, apples, peanuts, sugarcane, or sawdust.

How to Select Household Livestock

WHAT CONSTITUTES A PET?

Generally, men gauge the value of pets by balancing the food value of the animal with the Keanelike softness of the animal's eyes. Goats are more charming than many dogs. But we can look into Fido's eyes and see loyalty, affection, faithfulness, adoration—all the qualities we long for in friends, women, and animals. If you look into a goat's eyes, you go mad. The devil has eyes like a goat's. So we eat goats and play tug-of-war with dogs. Cows have the best eyes, but most of us just can't get around our deep desire for burgers. Someplace, however, we do draw the line between friends and dinner. In France, for example, they eat the roasts upon which we ride down long, dusty trails, and in the Far East, people use the noggins of our simian cousins as a kind of brain-pan dip-dish.

For most of us, though, we just need a way of distinguishing a good pet from a lousy one. Therefore, the modest question of what constitutes a pet is freighted with sexual meaning and a kind of anthropological dialectic.

We can't know with any certainty how women feel about pets. But we know what men like. Historically, when most guys who counted were Egyptians, we thought cats were the paradigm pet. Goes to show how far we've come, yes? A hundred years ago, the pet of choice was a horse. Today, the base unit of pet equivalency for modern men is the dog. Once you understand what a good dog is worth, the value of all other animals becomes relative to the value of one good dog. It's like knowing what an Italian *lira* is worth, or a Polish *zloty*. **If you know the value of one good dog, you can calculate the value of almost any other pet.** For example:

HOW TO TELL THE DIFFERENCE BETWEEN A BEEF COW AND A DAIRY COW: HINT: DAIRY COWS GIVE MILK

From this chart we can see why more women than men are vegetarians, since many of the animals women consider cute are considered by

STANDARD DOG CONVERSION CHART

1 ficus	=	.003 Dog
1 chicken	=	.050 Dog
1 parakeet	=	.200 Dog
1 hamster	=	.250 Dog
1 cat	=	.330 Dog
1 bunny	=	.400 Dog
1 lamb	=	.600 Dog
1 cow	=	.700 Dog
1 mutt from the pound	=	1.00 Dog
1 border collie	=	1.20 Dogs
1 horse	=	1.40 Dogs
1 mule	=	1.70 Dogs
1 monkey	=	2.300 Dogs

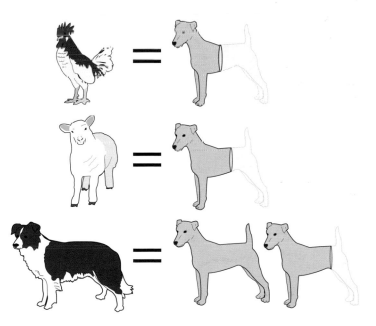

men to be mighty good eating. However, as we can also see from this chart, the pets we normally associate with women are generally worth less than one good dog, while all masculine pets are worth at least a dog, and sometimes more. The question of how many men are equal to one good dog is left unanswered, however.

How to Teach an Old Dog New Tricks

No corporal education: There're two ways to train your dog—the right way or any number of wrong ways. Wrong ways include yelling at your dog when he doesn't do a trick the way you want him to, hitting him when he doesn't do the trick the way you want it done, rewarding him every once in a while during the training session just because he's still hanging around while you put him through all of this ridiculousness.

Good Dog, Bad Dog

Canine ed done the right way is called positive reinforcement, which means every time your dog does something right during a training session—no matter how small a movement toward the right behavior it is—you reward him. *Under no circumstances do you reward him for any other behavior.* If you do, you ruin the effect of all previous training because with an unearned reward you will be reinforcing some behavior (or no behavior, if you give your dog a treat simply for lying there looking cute) other than the behavior you want.

If you're beginning to see that training your dog takes some training of you first, you're catching on fast. Therefore, before we start working on your dog, let's start working on you.

Good Master, Bad Master

What you have to train yourself to do before you can train your dog is to learn to look at the trick you want your dog to do as a trick made up of many mini-tricks. In other words, **you have to see the trick the way your dog sees it.** Think of training your dog the way you learned to water-ski. Your instructor didn't throw you off the boat with two skis and tell you to grab the rope and hold on. No, he explained how to put the wet suit on. How to put the skis on, how to get into the water with the skis on, how to lie on your back while you wait for the rope to come around, how to grab the rope, how to hold the rope, how to get into position, how to put your feet when the boat starts to pull you, what to do when you get up—and what to do when you fall down. You learned to water-ski by mastering hundreds of little tasks along the way. And your positive reinforcement? The guy driving the boat telling you you were doing great even though you were getting your butt dragged all over the lake without success. The smile of the pretty girl in the bikini who was sitting in the back of the boat watching you and waiting for her turn. Finally, the ultimate reinforcement was that you finally got up.

The Fetch Trick

Want to teach your dog to fetch? First, figure out which different tricks together constitute your basic fetch: Watching the stick fly through the air, noticing where it lands, running to the stick, picking it up, running toward you with it, dropping it at your feet.

- *Grab your bag of treats and a stick.* Hang on to the treats and throw the stick and yell "Fetch!" If your dog makes no move toward the stick, your neighbors will think you're nuts. But who cares? You know they've been trained to think that way.
- *If your dog makes any kind of move toward the stick, reward him.* If he doesn't move toward the stick, go to where the stick landed and give your dog a treat if he follows you all or part of the way. Repeat this, getting him closer and closer to the stick and rewarding him, then start rewarding him only when he moves toward the stick without needing you to lead him.
- *Pick-up sticks.* Some dogs chase a stick, but they never pick it up. If this is your dog, go with him to the stick, pick it up, and put it near his mouth. If he takes it, he gets a treat. If not, you have to break picking up the stick into smaller pieces. Try offering the treat and the stick at the same time. Eventually, he will get the point.

HOW TO BUST A BRONC

Sometimes the slow trot of a man's life turns into something else. That's when you decide either to take control or ride it out.

When you're working with an unfamiliar and unbroken horse, make sure all your moves are smooth and confident. Try to rein in your nervousness before you try to rein in the horse, who will be nervous enough for both of you. And remember to work slowly and patiently: Some of these steps have to be repeated for days. The routine about jumping on a wild-eyed stallion and staying there until he cries "Uncle!" is movie stuff.

1. ***First moves:*** Assuming the horse is accustomed to the halter, snub the horse tightly to a solid wall at least seven feet high. Teach the horse to move its hind end from left to right, first with the use of a whip (if necessary) along with voice commands, until voice commands alone do the job.

2. ***Sitting on the horse:*** Once the horse will follow your voice commands, calmly and confidently approach the horse on the *left* side and climb on. Sit quietly until the horse accepts your weight. If the horse is snubbed tightly to the wall, he can't throw you, but use caution, as this is a critical moment for both the horse and the rider. Remain on the horse until you feel him relax under you.

HOW TO MAKE A BIRD TALK

Nowhere but in bird education is the true value of conversation revealed, where you discover that what you put into the art of discourse is delivered back to you with interest. So invest wisely.

- ***The bird boom:*** Once upon a time, every boy had a dog. But then most of America moved into town, and the world of pets went to the birds. People are now flocking to birds.
- ***If elephants spoke:*** One major reason for birds' popularity is that people like to own animals that will talk back to them. For most people, cats and dogs have a very limited vocabulary, while most birds—cute, easy to care for, and relatively inexpensive—will converse readily.
- ***Stoolies:*** Talking birds are sensitive to their environment. As these birds mature from babies to adults, they bond to people. Sometimes, they even adopt people as their substitute mates. And in order to communicate with their "mates," they talk.
- ***Learning curve:*** Most birds can learn to chatter until they are approximately two years old. If the bird hasn't talked by then, he probably won't—a real downer if your bird is a cockatoo with an eighty-eight-year life span.

"Relaxation" is an important word for bird teachers to learn, since a calmer bird is likely to be a chattier bird. Try these tips:

- *Keep baby birds close to the ground* until they develop balance skills.
- Cultivate your own balance skills by making sure you give your bird a *nutritionally balanced diet* with foods of varying texture, color, and shape.
- Never let anyone handle your bird roughly.
- *Avoid fast, sudden movements* that might frighten your bird.
- *Can birdie say, "The pen of my aunt is on the table?"* If you're having trouble getting a young bird to talk to you, try picking up a learn-to-talk CD from a pet shop. Just fifteen minutes a day of one of these Berlitz-for-the-birds tapes should stimulate your parrot to eloquent discourse. An untried experiment: a Stephen King audio book.
- *Keep your emotional life out of your bird's face.* Why? Because no matter how old the bird is, if his environment is unpleasant, he will shut up and speak nevermore.
- *A special tip for men.* Talking birds are more responsive to a female voice, so it helps to get one, if you can. On the other hand, if you're a single guy and you can't get girls to talk to you, you shouldn't expect much from a parrot either.

Ten Steps into the Woods

Okay. You know where you are. You know where you want to be. But there's a lot a man should know before he leaves hearth and home and heads off into unlisted real estate. If you stop to look it all up now, you'll never get out of the house. Instead, just head out, taking it one step at a time:

1. FIND A PATH

- ***And stay on it.*** If you're in a wilderness area used extensively for recreation, do everything possible to stay on the paths that have been made by others. The less off-path hiking you do, the better the wilderness will be for everybody coming along behind you.
- ***Stay off it.*** If you're in a real wilderness—the pristine, untouched kind—your path through the woods must be as invisible after you've passed as it was before you arrived.
- ***Mark it well.*** If you're inexperienced, mark a path. Al Gore, the enviroveep, just after his election, took a walk in the woods and promptly got lost. For hours. It took the Secret Service to steer him along the right path. Don't count on their help, though, unless you've got Tipper in the tent. Instead, watch where you're going—really watch—and stop frequently to acquaint yourself with your surroundings. Remember, on your way into the woods, you'll be seeing everything that's behind you when you're on your way back out again. If you can follow that sentence, you can follow a track through the trees. Boy Scouts are taught to break stems on pathside plants and make small knife-cuts along the way.

  If you get lost in the woods—or anywhere out-of-doors, for that matter—find an animal path, a deer trail, a cattle lane, or any obvious cut made by animals. Follow this to water. Then follow the water downstream. You'll eventually come to civilization. If you follow the water upstream, you'll get farther away from settlements.
- ***Make your own way.*** If you really want to get serious about marking a path, though, blaze the whole damn trail yourself. Start small, and move up to the big stuff.

How to Use a Machete

Think Sampras: Machetes are dangerous if used improperly, said one knife-wielding pathfinder. Think backhand, backhand, backhand.

Use the machete as it goes away from you. Never use a forehand. When you swing a machete, don't do it so the end of your swing has you as the target. Remember, backhand only. And if you're working with other guys, you should work more or less back to back, not side by side. That's obvious, yes?

How to Fell a Tree

Think Bunyan: If you get tired whacking the small stuff, go for that ugly-big redwood blocking your path. Here's how one correspondent chain-saws his way through all that annoying old-growth:

- *You first notch the tree* on the side you want it to fall on. You've got a tree standing there vertically, and if you want it to fall to the right, you've got to saw a notch in there to the right.
- *You cut it about halfway through,* and angle it down at forty-five-degrees, take the notch out and then go to the other side and start cutting opposite the notch, and just slightly below it, and the tree will fall into the notch.
- *You try not to make it fall downhill,* because if you do that, you have to carry all the wood back up.
- *Then you limb it,* and then, if you've got a stove that holds eighteen-inch wood, you saw it up into eighteen-inch lengths.
- *Then you take your ax and split it,* and you throw it in the truck, stack it, and let it dry out so you can burn it in the winter.

Today, you use a chain saw to do the cutting, but in the old days we used an ax because there weren't any chain saws. So we chipped a notch and then started cutting on the other side. But using an ax is sort of like flying: You've got to have awareness. You've got to know what's going on around you.

2. WALK THE WALK

First off, recognize the **Main Thing** *about hiking: your feet.* Are they healthy? Toenails trimmed? No fungus?

Next, **you have to dress your feet for outdoor use.** Two things to keep in mind about what you keep on your feet: Keep 'em light and keep 'em dry.

Let's say you're a regular guy going out for some regular hiking or regular camping or regular backpacking. Don't get fancy. Buy a pair of medium-weight trail boots. They're as easy to find as a pair of athletic shoes. The **Main Thing:** comfort. If they feel good, give them a once-over to make sure they're made well. Buy them. Hit the trail.

On the other hand, if you plan on putting your new boots to much more demanding tests, consider the following:

- *The fit counts.* To get a good fit: Go to a good boot shop. Make sure you wear the same socks to the store that you will wear in the woods.

  Here's what you're looking for: *A snug fit around the ball of your foot and across the instep.* You shouldn't have to achieve this by yanking at the laces.

  To test for the snugness of the fit, do the following: Stand up. Have a friend or the salesman wrap a hand around the instep of the boot with one hand and squeeze—if you've got a snug fit, you're in good shape. If there's lots of extra room in there, you're going to be flying all over the place inside that boot while you walk. Good way to grow blisters.

- *Talk to the salesman* before you try on a single pair. Does he look and sound like he knows what he's talking about?

- *Make sure he measures your feet* with a thing called a Brannock Device. This is important: The Brannock will give you a better measurement than anything else on the planet. Might not be too important to you when you're buying penny loafers to wear to work, but then, at work you probably don't walk twenty miles a day with sixty pounds strapped onto your back. In addition to measuring the length and width of your foot with great precision, the Brannock will measure ball-to-heel length, which is a crucial factor in boot fit. Ask your salesman to explain it to you—but if he can't, hoof it.

- *If one foot is larger than the other,* buy to fit the larger foot.
- *Walk on an incline* to judge whether your toes are going to slam into the front of the boots when you go downhill. You've got to have enough room that your toes don't hit the tip of the boots, but not so much room that your toes slide around.
- *How heavy are the boots?* Weight really counts. You want to avoid buying the heaviest boots in the store. After all, you will pick them up and set them down thousands of times every day. Why add weight you don't need to be dragging around?
- *Keep walking around the store.* Be patient. Walk around. Walk some more. Bend over. Do a squat thrust. Stand on a bench using only the toes of the boots. Put them to a test before you leave the store. Still feel good? Okay, maybe you've found the boots for you.

3. DRESS FOR THE OCCASION

This is a walk in the woods, lads, not a stroll on the boardwalk. If you're heading up and not down, remember that for every one thousand feet in elevation you climb, the temperature will drop 3 to 5 degrees. Like, if you're at Newport Beach and you're walking to the top of Everest, take a coat because it's 150 degrees cooler looking eye-to-eye with K2 than it is watching the babes in the pipeline.

Always keep a hat, sunglasses, and sunscreen handy.

If it's a warm-weather walk, bring T-shirts, shorts, hat with brim, long-sleeve turtleneck, sweatshirt with hood, ski cap or other hat for cold and nighttime use, lightweight pants, lightweight long-sleeved shirt, rain poncho, bandanna.

If you're hiking through the cold, steely marches of Minnesota, wear your clothes in three layers—depending on how long you're going and how much you can carry. Why three layers instead of one garment that keeps you warm and keeps you dry? Maximum flexibility. Take it off, put it on.

The Three Layers

1. *Wear polypropylene* or an equivalent lightweight polyester knit like Capilene or Thermax against your skin, as if it were long underwear. These are light and warm, and they wick moisture away from your skin.

2. *A pile or fleece polyester jacket or pullover.* This is the stuff you see inside casual jackets that looks like a high-pile terry cloth. This is strictly for warmth, although it also helps wick moisture away.

3. *The last layer protects you from the rain.* Make sure the garment you choose is made of Gore-Tex or an equivalent. These fabrics have pores big enough to breathe and let your sweat out, but the pores are smaller than water so the rain can't come in.

Hats and Headbands

One thing that can be a lifesaver is the hat you wear. Some guys prefer a fleece headband that covers their ears and keeps heat from escaping from their head, but lets them feel the fresh cool air on the top of their noggin. If the top of your head gets cold, you can throw on anything from a ski cap to a baseball cap over the headband to keep the top of your head warm, too. This layered approach gives you the same maximum flexibility that you'll need in connection with your other clothing.

A dissent: Always cover the top of your head, as well as your ears, since up to half your body heat escapes through your head—bald or not bald. Believe it or not, no matter what part of your body is cold, covering your head will help take the chill off.

What Not to Wear

You don't want to wear cotton—with the exception of cotton T-shirts. *Cotton is no friend to the backpacker.* When it gets wet, it doesn't keep you warm anymore; plus, it gets heavy and it takes a long time to dry.

Wool, on the other hand, does take a long time to dry and does get heavy, but at least it will keep you warm while the drying process is in progress.

4. CARRY YOUR OWN FREIGHT

Camping is the one form of travel where your carry-ons really do count. Once upon a time, a chap could tie up all his rations in a hankie, tie it to a stick, and down the road he went. The evolutionary chain is familiar: Metal-and-canvas back breakers gave way to aluminum-and-nylon Quasimodo boxes. Now, we have *internal* backpacks. Progress.

- *Internal packs* have padded struts built right into them. These supports are generally better molded to the body. They fit better on your back and shoulders, too, especially compared to the aluminum external frame back packs, which required your back and shoulders to adjust to them.

- *External frame packs* have an upside too, though. First, there's the cost. You also get more pockets: There are both main compartments and little ones on the exterior. It may seem like a minor point now, while you're sitting there drinking your coffee, but when you're out in the woods and you need toilet paper *bad,* and you have an internal frame pack with only one internal compartment and one external compartment and you can't find the toilet paper, you might feel differently. External frame packs generally have two main compartments and little pockets all over the place. Smart backpackers with external frames, by the way, generally keep the essentials like TP and water close hand in the same out side, easy-to-reach pocket on every trip.

  Rule of thumb: External backpacks are better for storage; internals are better for carrying.

5. HOME IS WHERE YOU PITCH IT

Most men start their tenting careers under a blankie thrown up between two kitchen chairs. Then we get testosterone and move out.

- *Two views of life outside.* Might as well talk about this now, since it's going to come up eventually. See, the downside of camping is exactly the same as the downside of losing a war. So you can call it camping if you want but history has another word for it.

- *This is where tents come in,* and this is also where we turn a corner on how we can look at the whole sleep-and-eat-outside

How to Check into God's Motel: These are the most modern versions of the three tent types most commonly used: Two-man "pup" tent, with poles. One- or two-man tent with external supports. Family wall tent, with external supports.

experience. New-model tents are to camping what federal low-security prisons are to the corrections business. They're practically luxurious, plus they seem to float off the ground: They're almost freestanding—with a delicate filigree of ropes and pegs added almost as an afterthought—and they take about three minutes to set up and take down.

How to Set up a Modern Tent

The new tents are dome shaped. Along the outer or inner perimeter of the dome are small slits through which you slide two or more poles. Around the base of the tent, there are fittings that hold the ends of the poles. **The inertia of the bent poles around the outside of the dome holds the tent up and in place.** You may wish to sturdy your tent by putting a few pegs around the outside of it, but in most cases this is unnecessary—your weight and the weight of your gear alone will keep the tent from blowing away.

Tents Come Rated by Season

There are two-weather tents, three-weather tents, and four-weather ones. Obviously, a four-weather tent is the postman's delight. It'll get you through the worst rain, the deepest snow, the coldest sleet, and the darkest gloom of night. For the vast majority of us, a four-weather tent is overkill. **A three-weather tent will get you through almost anything but severe winter.** A two-weather tent is really a one-weather tent: You use it on a warm nights where you want to get away from the chill and the bugs and maybe a light summer rain. It's as close as you can get to sleeping under the stars naked.

Two Ways to Wet

There are two sources of water inside a tent. One source is, of course, outside: It rains, tent leaks, you're wet.

The other source is inside: Some tenting material is waterproof, all right, but that which seals the water out, also traps condensation in. The principle of staying dry in a tent is very much the same as the principle of staying dry in your clothes: The two secret words are "layering" and "wicking." The layering comes in the form of the tent, which should be made of a porous polyester material that will let your body heat out and mostly not let the rain in. Now, over the tent, you put a waterproof rain fly, which not only keeps rain out but also traps moisture as it escapes through the tenting. You're the furnace in a good tent.

The other crucial thing to look for in a tent: Tub construction or a floor that continues partway up the walls in one piece. Without tub construction, it is a lot easier for water to run into your tent.

Where to Pitch the Tent

The ideal location is a slight incline someplace far from the site of any potential flooding. If you camp on perfectly flat ground, you'll be vulnerable to water in the event of rain. Pitch the tent so your head is higher than your feet and avoid sleeping across a slope because you will spend all night trying to keep yourself from rolling into the wall of your tent.

Pitching a tent under a tree can have a few advantages—provided you're sure the tree is strong and sturdy. One advantage is that you will have shade for part of the day, so your tent will stay nice and cool in the daytime hours. Meanwhile, if it rains you will be partly protected from the rain. If you like looking at the stars at night, don't camp under a tree with too much foliage. Watch out for lightning.

If the site allows it, handpick the view you will see out your tent door. It might be wise to anticipate the weather; if you suspect rain, avoid pointing your tent's door into the storm. Pointing your tent to the south or east will give you the morning sun, which can be a real bonus. Avoid trying your guy-lines to weaker branches of a tree—in a storm or heavy winds they will whip around and so will you. On the other hand, if you think wind will play a heavy hand in the night's weather, consider pitching your tent up against a fallen log or large rock or other natural element that can serve as a windbreak.

Tent Tips

- ***Don't cook*** in your tent unless you want to die. Tents aren't fire-proof, and even if fire didn't get you, lack of oxygen might.
- ***If you use a candle lantern in your tent,*** make sure you set it on a solid flat surface in a place where you won't kick it. Better yet, figure out a way to hang it so it is impossible to knock it down or against the wall of the tent.
- ***Take a ground cloth***—it'll keep water out if you have any holes in the floor of your tent. The other great thing about a ground cloth: It keeps the bottom of your tent clean. Let's face it, you can throw a ground cloth away when it gets so dirty you just can't stand it. Tents, on the other hand, cost a heck of a lot more money.
- ***Pack your poles and stakes separately*** from your tent to avoid puncturing it. Always carry a few extra poles.
- ***Always take a piece of ripstop nylon*** and a repair kit with you.
- ***Seal the seams of your tent with a waterproofing agent*** the first time you set it up and the first time you use it after a long hiatus. If your tent is going to leak, the seams are one of the main places it will do so.
- ***Clean your tent immediately*** after you get home from a trip. Once you put it back in the garage, you'll never do it and it will smell like a gym locker the next time you go to use it. As part of the cleaning, open all the flaps and allow it to air out.

6. WEAR A BEDROOM SUITE

Think of a sleeping bag as a big, ugly suit. You can make yourself happy if you just get one that fits.

Mummy Bags Keep You Warmer

Sleeping bags keep you warm because they are designed to keep the air warm around your body. You bring in the heat, the bag keeps it there for you. Mummy bags are smaller and snugger, so there is less air to heat, less air to keep heated. You stay warmer. Also, the rectangular bag has a large opening, thus more cold air can get in. The mummy bag has a hood that keeps the warm air from escaping. The hood of a mummy prevents heat loss because your head is actually inside the bag and only your face is exposed if you draw the opening of the hood tight. On really cold nights, you may want to leave just your nose exposed. Still, the roomier ambiance of a rectangular bag has some virtue and you can ditch that, too, if you can squeeze another person inside with you.

7. PLUMBING

You know, nothing dresses up a john like a big bouquet of red oaks and poison ivy.

- *First, find a spot at least two hundred feet front your site,* and from any body of water—lake, stream, creek, river, ocean. If you're smart, you'll make it at least two hundred feet downwind from your campsite and the trail, too. Failure to abide by this rule will result in the sudden appearance of paper rangers from the local EPA office, who will drop out of the trees and haul you off to federal court. In 1995, the EPA helped throw a seventy-four-year-old apple farmer in the clink for the rest of

his life for messing up the paperwork it made him do to monitor how much of his cider waste went into the local creek. The EPA is not busy. So a lone figure such as your very self, out in the woods with serious mien and small shovel, looks like a dream come true for an enviro-dink. Therefore, do it right or do it for five to life.

- *Dig a small hole.* Make it no larger than necessary: If you're a normal guy, maybe eight inches across. If you're an academic, you might need several extra feet in both directions. Eight inches is the magic depth; at that level there are lots of little microorganisms that will actually thank you for the treat. Do your duty. Use septic-safe toilet paper sparingly. If you're really worried about the larger environment, don't use any at all. This will cause others to express concern about your own personal environment. Bury your work.
- *Traveling in packs?* If there is a big group of you, dig a trench latrine. Same rule about the depth, just dig it wide. After each use, you should sprinkle enough dirt over the waste to keep away the flies.
- *Don't feed the animals.* Don't bury anything else in the latrine, like dishwater and leftover food, since animals may be attracted to the smell of your food. The contamination can cause death.
- *Dishwater and food scraps.* Make a separate kitchen latrine. Follow the same rules as above. Use biodegradable soap to wash dishes. Use as little water as possible.

8. KAMP KITCHEN

The Fire

Making a cooking fire is not an instinctive business for a man. Especially under difficult circumstances, building a good, useful fire is a lot like courtship: You have to coax it along, bit by bit, for if you try to get too much heat too quickly, you'll only snuff it out.

- *Always build your fire on rock or dirt.*
- *Clear the area at least three feet* in all directions of the fire site of all flammable material.
- *Start with the smallest pieces of fuel*—tinder and kindling—and then work up to larger and larger pieces of fuel until you have your logs burning. Here's the sequence: a yank of thread, a few leaves,

a *match,* a handful of twigs, some small branches, a few small logs—maybe something about as big around as your wrist—then a couple of larger logs. Take it slow, and stack your fire in a loose pyramid. These principles apply to all types of fires.

- *Make sure your fire gets plenty of oxygen.* The rule here is that the amount of air, not the amount of fuel, controls the heat of a fire.
- *The "hunter's fire."* This is a good, general-purpose fire, useful for both cooking and heating. Start by digging a shallow fire pit with two close rows of rocks or green logs on two sides parallel to one another and parallel to the wind, while the other two sides remain open. Build your fire in the pit between the rocks, which provide a place to set your pots and pans over the fire so your food can cook without sitting directly in the fire. With two sides open that face and oppose the wind, air is allowed to come in one side of the pit and leave through the other open side, thus fanning the fire and keeping it hot and also providing a lot of heat at the side where the warmed air comes out. If you want to control the fire, you can use a windbreak of rocks at one end as a kind of damper.
- *Fuel.* The wood you burn will determine whether you have a good wood for cooking or for staying warm. The rule of thumb: The drier and harder the wood, the hotter the fire. Give your fire some time before you start cooking. The coals are hotter than the flames, so when it comes to cooking and heating, the coals are far more important.
- *A happy-camper clean-up tip.* Rub soap over the outside of your pot before you start cooking. When you are done, the soap will rinse right off and so will the black from the fire.

9. TOOLS OF THE TRAIL

If your foray into Nature is a day trip, this will be an awesome exercise in overpack. But if your trip has a four-day/three-night, single-occupancy feel to it, this is your checklist.

- **First-aid and survival kit,** which includes:

    For day hikes, take matches, compass, whistle, moleskin, toilet paper, some kind of antigerm spray or cream, sunscreen, aspirin, insect repellent, Band-Aids, a first-aid booklet, a quarter or two for a phone call, and a cell phone.

For casual camping, bring all of the above plus tweezers, needle for blisters, razor blade, Tums, Alka-Seltzer, Pepto-Bismol, Ace bandage, a compress, scissors, gauze and tape, and a triangular bandage.

- *For backpacking,* You need to anticipate every problem, then find a set of very small solutions. Usually, you can find all of the things above, only in miniature. (Okay, except the Ace bandage.) Also, make sure you take some fishing line, hooks, safety pins, a mirror.
- **Stove.** If you don't want to build a fire—or if fires aren't permitted in your neck of the woods—tote a small stove. The gas canisters are cheap and they produce a lot of heat pronto. That's good news when you're cold and want nothing more than a hot cup of coffee.
- **Water bottle.** Two choices here: You can blow a sawbuck at Al's Owl World and pick up a water bottle, or you can spend a buck-twenty-nine and grab a big bottle of water at the 7-Eleven. Buy a big one to keep filled with water in your pack, and a smaller one to keep near at hand.

  Three more water tips:

1. *When on the trail,* don't ever drink the last of your water—you don't know, for sure, when you'll get more.
2. *These days, take no chances:* Purify all water unless you're in a state or federal park and you are told specifically that the water is safe to drink.
3. *When it is* really *cold,* stuff your water down into your back, wrapped in clothes, to keep it from freezing.

- **Sunglasses and hat.** Make sure the glasses are UV-safe. The best hats don't make your head itch after a while, so that rules out anything lined with polyester.
- **Shovel.** Go for the avalanche shovel at your local backpacking shop. It's light, doesn't take up much room. Lightweight alternative: a small plastic trowel.
- **The right socks.** That means two layers. A wicking sock first, which is usually made of polypropylene. These socks draw moisture off your feet and into the heavier socks you are wearing over

them. Make your second pair of socks wool or polypropylene, depending on the weather. Avoid cotton socks: Unlike wool or polypropylene, which will keep your feet warm even when wet, cotton socks will just make your feet cold when they get wet—and they will, even if you're no place near water.

- **Flashlight.** Bring extra batteries.
- **Pocketknife.**
- **Rope.**
- **Poncho.** The standard GI poncho is a piece of genius with a hole in it. It's great because it gives a full range of motion with your arms while being long enough in back to cover both you and the top portion of your pack in the rain.
- **Tube tent.** A "tube tent" is a piece of lightweight plastic. Emergency? Tie a rope between two trees, drape the plastic over the rope and you're home. Takes about two minutes to unpack and put up. Throw it on the ground, and you have a great ground cloth. Cheap, too.

10. LIVING OFF THE LAND

Specifically, that thin margin of land adjoining a highway. We received an alarming number of correspondence on the subject of road kill, most of which bore an if-you're-going-to-hit-it, you might as well eat-it kind of sensibility.

These recipes are too disgusting to belabor, but in the interests of thoroughness, we're providing two to tide you over until the meat wagon comes.

Note: Freshness is everything here. If you need a tool to get your dinner off the road, you may as well face the fact that you're dealing with food well past its prime.

Skin 'em. All road kill must be skinned and cleaned. The mere presence of tire tracks does not render a carcass pot-ready. For most small animals, make incisions around the neck, down the belly, and around the haunches. Then peel back the skin. Eviscerate the animal. Remove the head and tail.

Parboil 'em. All crushed critters need to be soaked in water long enough to bleach the blood out of the meat. Then the carcass must be parboiled—in which the meat is plunged into boiling water long enough to begin the cooking process. To the water you should add salt—more than you think you need—and pepper and whatever other stuff amuses you: red peppers, celery, onions, whatever's handy.

RABBIT

Cut the rabbit up into pieces. Trim along the ribs and back, and remove the rear legs.

Put all the pieces in a pot and parboil until the meat is tender.

Fry the pieces in a skillet with plenty of pepper. You can roll the pieces in flour first, if you have some handy.

POSSUM

Soak the skinned animal overnight.

Parboil the intact carcass—minus the charming head and that very attractive ropelike tail—until tender. Add plenty of salt and pepper.

Bake the thing until it's done. You can add yams or turnips to the baking pan, if you wish. In fact, the possum would no doubt have liked it that way.

How to Avoid Giving Blood

Mosquitoes are like kids. The minute they stop making noise, you know they're into something, like your circulatory system. A lazy guy with a fishing pole—or any man outdoors—is nothing but a big hunk o' bait for a mosquito. Here's how to avoid those needle-nosed nibblers:

- ***Unplug the zapper.*** Bug zappers have almost no ability to reduce the number of skeeters. They sure aren't any good for keeping them away, since they work by attracting the bugs they kill. Many bugs are thus left unzapped. Best bet: Get your neighbor to buy one.

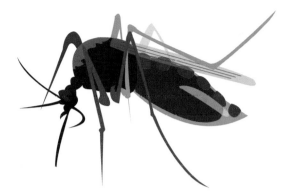

- *Avon's Skin-So-Soft Moisturizing Suncare.* Hey, big guy, go sensitive with the help of the door-to-door lady. This stuff contains citronella, a mild and natural repellent.
- *DEET.* It's hard to beat this as a repellent, but use it sparingly. The stuff is potent enough to eat through your parka, and it's been known to cause eye and skin problems. Go for a 20 percent concentration; you'll get the same protection as you would with the pure stuff, but with a lot less risk.
- *Skeeter hats.* The kind with the mesh veil cost around three bucks and work like a charm. Mosquitoes see you coming in one of those camobridal veils, and they run away laughing. Good riddance.

How to Charm a Snake

Snakes are nearly blind. But they obsess on what they do manage to see. Since they detect motion easily, you can draw a snake's attention away from you or your boot by getting it to pay attention to the tip of a moving stick. This is the same principle used in India by snake charmers. They get the snake to follow the moving object—usually the tip of a flute or whistle—and rise out of the basket. If the cobra strikes, it strikes the flute, not the flutist.

SNAKE BITES

Good boots can make the difference between a snake attack and a snake bite.

Good sense is what you'll need if you're snake-bit. Three tips:

1. **Stay calm.** Panic causes your heart to pump, and that speeds the venom to your heart.
2. **Don't move.** You don't want to increase demands on your circulatory system. If you must walk, take it slow and easy.
3. **Get to a medic.** Carving up the bite and sucking out the poison only leaves you with a mouth full of poisonous blood. Almost all snake-bit guys can survive a trip even to a remote medical facility where antivenom can be obtained.

How to Outwit Fish

A trout is a fish. Fish have brains so small that fish neurosurgeons have to do their work under electron microscopes. So why, then, are so many smart men outwitted by so many dim fish? The answer to this ancient and vexing question may be found in the secret book read only by successful salesmen, right there in the section called "You Gotta Know the Territory." For a trout, the territory is a small stretch of streambed. A chap hoping to sell a trout the goods at the end of his line has to know the territory as well as his client does. Otherwise, no sale. Here's how to close:

- **Find a good stream to fish.** The best trout streams have several similar characteristics: They have a relatively subtle gradient—sometimes as little as a fifty- to seventy-five-foot drop over the course of a mile; you will not catch trout in waterfalls. They have a reliable source of cold water—a spring or a neighborhood glacier. They have a clean streambed—lots of rocks and gravel, not much sand and silt. And all good trout streams have a lot of good things for trout to eat in them.

- **In the morning, fish small areas of white water**—riffles—and shallow areas of slow flow—flats—since those are the parts of a stream where trout go for breakfast.

- *In the afternoon, fish shady banks and deep pools.* Not only do these features provide an angler with a little midday shade, they are also ideal cool-water dives for lunching trout.
- *In the evening,* you can either return to a favorite riffle or find some decent "pocket" water—the deep, calm plunge pools at the bottom of a rapids or the shallow eddies behind large boulders.

FIVE MAINSTREAM TRUTHS

1. The current in the middle of a stream is four times as fast as the current near the banks.
2. The faster the water, the smaller the fish.
3. There's more trout food on a rocky bottom than on a sandy one.
4. The patterns of a 25-foot-wide trout stream—flats, riffles, pools—repeat every 150 feet or so.
5. Trout see you long before you see them; an aspiring angler has to stay below a 10 percent angle of vision to avoid being seen by lounging trout.

HOW TO FISH WITH FLIES

There are only two good reasons for a man to stand in water up to the point where, if you'll excuse me, men's health is an issue. Fixing pipes is one. Catching fish is the other.

Leaking overflows, flooded basements, busted drains, all call for a big-money fix. But unlike plumbing, a skill practiced by extremely well paid tradesmen, fishing is pursued almost completely by amateurs. That's because fishing is an act of complete symbolic satisfaction for most men, who come by a taste for the sport when they are young. A five-year-old boy impaling a worm on a hook and dropping it in the water with the hope of reward is participating in a pursuit so intractably manly that invariably the kid gets hooked on fishing long, long before a fish gets hooked by the kid.

There are of course many ways to catch a fish, and of all of them, fly-fishing is the least efficient. Nets are faster, worms are easier. Taking a half inch of metal and some bird feathers and tossing it in the river is

not a practical proposition. Yet, it is to fly-fishing that most men, at some usually middle-aged point in their lives, are drawn. That's because fly-fishing, as a passionate pursuit, is best suited to men who have lived just enough life to recognize its limitations and its comic potential, and need some way to try to make sense of it all. In this respect, fly-fishing is natural therapy, a workout for real life, for no other activity so perfectly combines every skill a man needs in order to succeed at all that's important.

Sex, Seduction, and the Choice of Flies

Here's what it takes to catch a trout, fly-wise. You must first choose a fly that looks exactly like every trout's dream dinner. Trout are not experimental animals. Unlike some fish who will take a bite of a giant, shiny plastic thingamajig just to see what it is, trout only recognize the familiar as food. If mayflies are mating, and the air is thick with small, white fluffs of bug, then your fly must look like a mayfly or no trout will want it. And even that isn't good enough: It must look like a mayfly, and act like a mayfly—or, to be exact, a mayfly that has accidentally ditched at sea.

In order to mimic a mayfly in distress, it is essential that you be able to cast a nearly weightless, phony mayfly fifty feet into a likely pool and have the fly alight first, with the rest of the line following subtly, almost absently behind. If you do all that—figure out the menu, imitate its behavior, and present the whole thing with perfect delivery—then, possibly, a trout may strike your fly.

Non-fly-guys may need *a real-life parallel* here, so let's look at it the enterprise this way. Wendy is a beautiful flight attendant. She lives in Montana. So do several million trophy-sized rainbow trout. Your chances of snagging Wendy are considerably better than your chances of bumping into even one of those trout. For one thing, Wendy says she's "looking for the right man." None of the trout feel that way. For another, Wendy, already married and divorced once, says she's "a sucker for a good line." No trout in her family. In fact, the only thing fishing has going for it in this little comparison is that rejection generally occurs out of sight, so it seems as if it's nothing personal.

But it is. A nibbleless fly fisherman is a social failure, the kind of guy fish take one look at and roll their little lidless eyes. As most men instinctively know, a little practice can make the courtship of a trout a bit smoother.

How to Pick Up Fish

1. *Rig yourself a rod* (not a *pole*), go out back, stand at one end of the yard, and put a paper or plastic plate at the other. Surround the plate with a carpet of flattened trash bags.

2. *To properly cast a line,* imagine your casting arm is a clock's hour hand, where you're facing nine o'clock, and three o'clock is dead behind you.

3. *Pull out twenty feet or so of line* and lay it on the ground in a straight line in front of you, so the fly is pointing at the plate. Take ten or twenty more feet of line off the reel and let it dangle at your side.

4. *If you're a righty, hold the loose line in your left hand,* and with your right arm, move the rod slowly and rhythmically back and forth between ten o'clock and one o'clock, making sure that when it passes twelve o'clock, it's pointing straight up. Never go to nine, and keep away from two. As the rod moves, you'll see the line unfurl above your right shoulder like a giant silk thread, and you'll feel the tug of the line as centrifugal force works on it.

5. ***Keep the line from your right elbow*** to the tip of the rod as straight as possible until you develop a feel for what you're doing. Too much wrist too early will give you nothing but lots of tangled line in the nearby trees.

6. ***Work on the rhythm of the rod.*** Wait until the moment the line has unfurled behind you to begin your forward movement.

7. ***Release the line through your left hand*** a little bit at a time. Eventually, your line will play itself out.

8. ***When you feel like it, stop the rod at ten o'clock*** and watch where the fly goes. If it goes behind you, you have no sense of rhythm, and your casting motion needs a good backbeat. Most beginners go back and forth much too quickly. If it goes in front of you, you're halfway there. Once you've got the rhythm conquered, you'll want to try putting the fly in the plate. Remember, the sound you hear first should be the fly touching down on the platter. If you hear the line rustling on the trash bags, start over.

Line Control

Once you have the basic cast down, experiment with others. There are a million different ways to cast a line, but the key to all of them is getting a good feel for the peculiar dynamic of the rod and the line. For instance, a slight pull with the left hand on the line while the right arm is delivering forward thrust will give greater velocity to the line.

A Personal Observation:

You should be able to stand shoulder-to-shoulder with another fly fisherman and never know he's there. A good fly fisherman can land a fly on the water with all the impact of a whisper at Madison Square Garden.

Keeping track of your line and keeping your line under control are also useful skills. I used to fish with a guy who churned up the water as if he were using a small Moulinex at the end of his line. Guy married money, so he wore ten thousand dollars' worth of equipment, but he fished in a little sea of foam of his own manufacture. As an angler, he was extremely humane, in that he never caught fish, but he made it nearly impossible for those nearby to catch any, either.

Selling the Goods

You're the Willie Loman of the deep. You have to convince the trout your bug is the best bug. It's helpless, vulnerable, available, desirable. You have to get bug lust going big-time in a trout to get the fish to rise to the bait. How?

Know the market. When you get to trout-central, take a look before you go wading in. What kind of product is selling? Is there a rush on little, brown bugs with stiff wings, and no white mayflies anywhere? Then your white, fluffy mayfly is nowhere. Even if the trout spent the whole previous day eating mayflies, if yours is the only mayfly on offer, no self-respecting trout will touch it. Go for the brown-bug look. And watch the real thing as it floats on the surface. Is it a would be swimmer, making for dry land? Or is it resigned to its horrible fate, a listless, buoyant bite just waiting for the end? A typical trout wants what all its friends have, but better, so make your fly do the proper dance of death.

Closing the Deal

When a trout strikes, you'll lose him if you don't set the hook. Trout tend to inhale food rather than chomping down on it, and they'll exhale it just as fast if it doesn't feel right. When you see or feel the trout strike your fly, give a tiny tug. The effect is like the private eye knocking down the motel-room door with a camera in his hand. The trout says damn! and runs for it. **If the hook isn't set properly, the trout's out of there.** If you made the sale, there's a no-refund, no-return squabble on your hands, in which you let the trout wear himself out complaining as you slowly, slowly bring him in. Fly tackle is extremely lightweight stuff, so a panicky yank on your part will send the fish away with a souvenir.

Dress Appropriately

There are two really great things about fly-fishing gear. First, it's fun to own lots of it—all those strange tools, little pliers, gooey gels, vests, waders, flies galore. Second, you need almost none of it on any given day. Watch a guy with a heavy metal tackle box struggle along on a hot summer afternoon, and you'll appreciate the relative sparseness of fly tackle. If you look downstream and see a guy riding low in the water because he's heavy with gear, you're looking at a man who will only kill fish by falling on them. Plus, by not having to tote heavy equipment, you'll be free to self-decorate. Some guys, for example, would never dream of fly-fishing unless they were wearing a necktie. It's just a thing.

Remember, all you're doing is trying to outsmart fish and have some fun. Fly-fishing is not a noble calling. It's golf without holes, tennis without a net, basketball without the basket and without the ball. If you're a beginner, don't let yourself be intimidated by grizzled yuppies and ancient tweedsters. Just fish and admire the scenery.

Keeping Score

Should you be so incredibly lucky as to actually catch something trout-like, you'll have a new dilemma. Hard to believe, but some guys *fish for dinner.* If you reject all modern sensibilities, feel an excess of sanctimoniousness, find yourself more than an hour from a drive-through, or if you think the trout is a potential menace to navigation, you can take the monster back to camp and toss it in a skillet. If, however, you hope to be able to tell another angler about your good fortune, you must let the big one get away.

To touch a trout, first get your hand wet. Trout have no scales, and your dry hand will injure the trout's delicate skin.

- *Catch-and-release* may be seen in various lights: Perhaps it's just a way of introducing liberal guilt into a nearly guiltless enterprise. Or perhaps it's just simple good manners among experienced fly

fishermen who see the sport as a pedagogical exercise in which, with every encounter, both fisherman and fish gain in experience and wisdom, except the fish is the only one who actually swallows the hook. Either way, though, given the quickly growing number of men—and women—driven to snag trout on a feather, letting your trout swim free is perhaps the only way to make sure there are enough fish to go round. Catch-and-release is especially vital where efforts are being made to establish a native population; in many of these areas enlightened policies permit catch-and-release fishing only. Of course, *you can't hunt ducks this way,* but catch-and-release is the mark of a sporting angler who sees no need to lord it over a dying brookie.

So, Yankee flyboy, *how to prove you actually caught a trout?* Put your face and the fish's side by side in a camera viewfinder and pull the trigger. Wear a hat so you can tell who's who. You get to prove you caught a respectable fish; the fish gets to go home and tell his friends lies about how he got away from the big one.

HOW TO CATCH THE LAST TROUT OF THE SEASON

This, it must be said, is a piece of information you are *certain* you possess only when you have the last trout of the season actually on the end of your line. And it must be further admitted that for some of us, the first trout of the season is also the last trout of the season, and that for some unfortunate few, our "season" can be several years long.

Nevertheless:

- **Pressure drops:** First, no matter what part of the country you live in, *pay attention to the barometer.* Rapid falls or climbs can quickly start fish feeding or turn them off.
- **Worms work:** In rainy weather, *night crawlers will bring the last big trout out of hiding* in the cloudy water. If you're a fly-only fisherman, try beating the water with *oversized bass flies* during the last hour of daylight and during the first hour of evening.
- **Location, location, location:** Look for *rugged and inaccessible areas,* since these have the greatest likelihood of holding a trout population until the end of summer.

- *Use your noodle:* Finally, remember that by the time fall rolls around, the trout that remain alive have seen it all. They're like the best-looking women in a bar at closing time, and all the usual approaches are old hat to them by the time you show up with your tired old tricks. So don't be afraid to *vary your approach.* Try a different fly, some new bait, maybe explore a new river or lake.
- *In the Northeast:* Use *smaller lures* in shallow water as the bigger browns get ready to spawn upstream. Size-seven jointed Rapalas, floating bombers, bright colors fished slow and shallow seem to work best. Try small spoons worked under banks and around log jams to find those lingering giants.
- *For Western anglers:* Western fishermen should rely first on old favorites to finesse those lingering trout. For example, fly fishermen should *use a trusty woolybugger,* the M-16 of any fly fisherman's arsenal. If that doesn't work, *try a Zonker,* fished deep and with short, jerky retrieves. Still desperate? *Use live bait.* Sculpins and freshwater leeches are often overlooked by veteran anglers, but they can be quite deadly in the fall.

HOW TO CLEAN A CATFISH

Cats are kind of slick when you get them out of the water: They have skin instead of scales like most fish, and you can work yourself to death on a five-pound catfish just trying to hold on to him and skin him at the same time. They also have sharp little barbs beneath their gills. So you want to get the cat under control so you can work with it.

1. *Nail him to a stump.* The best way to skin a catfish is to find a stump and drive a nail through his head and into the stump. That'll stop the wiggling. Once you put the nail in his head, you pretty much took care of the old boy.
2. *Use your knife to cut around his neck.* You really want a good, sharp cut, so the skin comes off easy. But don't cut his head off, because if you cut his head off now, you've lost the use of your nail.
3. *Take your pliers and start skinning.* Now you see why you have to nail him to a stump. Otherwise, you can hardly hold him. Trying to keep hold of a catfish while you work is a miserable way to try

to skin one. You're trying to pull his skin off, and he's falling on the ground all the time. You really need a stump and a nail.

4. ***Gut him.*** Turn him over onto his belly. As a rule, you can start cutting him from the bottom and work your way toward his head, but you can do it either way. You just put your knife in there and rip the belly up as you go along. It's kind of like cutting a piece of cloth—once you get started, it just goes. Then reach your fingers in there and gut him—everything comes out. It's almost like it was meant to be that way; there's very little attachment there. A gutting rule of thumb: If it looks like something you don't want to eat, take it out.

   Once you do that, *then* you cut the head off. Now, you've got a good, clean catfish.

HOW TO CLEAN AND COOK A FISH THAT ISN'T A CATFISH

No stumps? No problem. There's more than one way to skin a fish. Good thing, too, since what you do with the fish immediately after you catch it will have a lot to do with how it will taste at dinner

- ***If the fish is alive,*** put him on a stringer and leave him in the water. Fish begins to decompose—giving it its customary smell—immediately after death.

- ***If the fish is badly injured*** and sure to die, clean your fish immediately and pack it in ice. The longer you wait before cleaning a dead fish, the better chance you have of the meat spoiling. The best way to pack a fish in ice is to wrap the fish up in watertight plastic bags and then put the bags on ice. This will keep the fish dry and fresh, while putting the fish directly in ice will make the flesh soft and mushy.

- ***Insert a sharp knife in the bottom of the fish,*** near where the body joins the tail, and slit forward to the V-shaped area where the belly meets the gills.

- ***Put your fingers into the gills*** and the V-shaped area, and pull downward toward the back of the fish, removing the gills and all of the innards.

- **Look inside your incision**—you will see a red line running up the back bone. It's blood. Beginning at the tail end of the fish, pierce this red line with your thumb, and run your thumb over the length of the fish until it has been removed.

Boneless Is Better
If you want fillets: Cut into the fish just behind the gills, cut down to the bone, then turn knife and slice through the fish along the backbone toward the tail.

- **Slice the fillet** away from the tail and the rest of the fish. Turn the fish over, and repeat the slice on the other side.
- **Remove the rib section**—again, using a knife with the blade flat and cutting along the ribs as close to the bone as possible.
- **Now remove the scales** by inserting the knife at the tail and cutting the skin away from the meat, taking care to waste as little as possible.

How to Hunt

Of all the things a man is asked to do, nothing else summons ancient instincts like the idea of hunting for food. Unlike changing a flat, running a chain saw, assembling a stock portfolio, or any other mundane

chore, hunting is the one thing we have in common with our oldest ancestors.

Trouble is—and maybe this is as emblematic as anything else of our disconnect from our elders—we no longer agree on how we feel about hunting. Some guys think it's just plain disgusting to stand on a hilltop and peek through the scope of a high-powered rifle at a doe-eyed doe on another hilltop a mile away and blast her to smithereens. Other guys can't imagine a better way to spend a day. Most of us are someplace in between, strung up like cheap Mexican ornaments between the eight-point antlers of ambivalence, lost in that perplexed dangle.

Let's take a look at both the upside and downside of hunting.

HUNTING PROS AND CONS

- *Guns are good.* The thing most guys like most about hunting is the firearms. If you hang in vaguely elitist circles and you just can't figure out what kind of a bumper sticker could ever shock the jaded guys you know down at the health club, join the NRA. The organization will send you a little three-inch disk you can slap right on your rear window. It reads, "Member—National Rifle Association." You put one of those babies on your Suburban and ride through the upmarket neighborhood of people who read the *New York Times,* and you generate serious apoplexy. It can be quite a rewarding feeling, actually.

But if you want to actually use the guns you own for hunting, you have to **consider the downside.** Here's a list of cautions:

- *Dork dress.* Listen, chaps, when Prince Philip and Prince Charles go out to cull the herds at Sandringham, they're dressed to kill. They wear lovely tweed hunting jackets, heavy twill trousers, really expensive boots, sweaters, and neckties, all in complementary earthtone shades. They are fully accessorized: They carry their guns with the same weathered nonchalance a veteran lawyer uses to tote his briefcase, and their field dogs trot along amiably. English hunters are like English landscapes: Philip and Charles make hunting look like an awfully decent way to spend a sunny, autumn afternoon, in which a man shoots game, drinks port, and discusses architecture with the maids. This is the England we all love, if only because cross-dressing isn't an unspoken part of the big picture. Even the dweebs of field death—fox hunters—looked damned swell in those lawn-jockey outfits, all mounted and surrounded by dogs, don't you think? All over Europe, hunters look this way, and not just because they have better taste than Americans—which, come on, they do—but also because when Euros go hunting, they don't do it in the suburbs, the way we do in America. When hunting season rolls around in America—and, most places, there's a season for all seasons—men go out in the forests of Appalachia and the Sierra looking like traffic cones, decked out in orange DayGlo Elmer Fudd hats and matching vests. Whether it's the first lovely spring day of turkey season, a midsummer's afternoon in the middle of groundhog season, or a crisp fall day on the opening day of buck season, there are thousands of stupid-looking guys in orange clothes wandering around the landscape with guns and hangovers. And speaking of handicaps: Americans who golf also love to hunt. Why? Wardrobe efficiency. The clothes some guys wear in the woods work perfectly well on the links. But who wants to be one of them?

- **Dork desperation.** In addition to dressing funny, a hunter must be willing to endure what to me is a massive dose of self-humiliation, self-discipline, and self-abuse in order to gain the upper hand over the local wildlife. For instance: A little garlic in your armpits or balsam fir needles in your pockets will help to disguise the smell of a human—a regular stench in any animal's book. Repels vampires, too. Plus, your after-hunting musk is going to drive women practically insane. What a hunting two-fer!

- **Hunter-general's warning.** One small upside of hunting is that even as you're trying to increase the health hazards to birds and animals, you can decrease your own, since you can't smoke while you're hunting. Deer can smell a smoldering butt a mile away. They can see it, too: Animals have sharp eyes and can easily spot that glowing cigarette and the sight of your smoke as it dissolves in the air around you, making you look mysterious, somewhat glamorous, a little dim, and terribly frightening.

- *The hills are alive with the sound of dying bunnies.* Here's something that works with animals that aren't deer: Dress up in your orange hat, grab a ghetto blaster, and go off into the woods with a full-blast tape of a dying rabbit. The woods are full of lazy animals with big appetites. Nothing combines these two characteristics like a rabbit in distress. Some good news: You don't have to make your own recording. You can buy a recording of Thumper's last moments, believe it or not, and if you play it while standing still at the edge of the woods anytime when food is hard to come by, you'll get lots of attention. Have a .22 handy or a 12-gauge.
- *The grocery impediment.* If you want to hunt for food, here are your choices: Either you can go down to Fred Sponsler's store and buy inch-point-five rib eyes, marinate them in garlic and beer, and toss them on a hickory fire, or you can bag a 150-pound buck down in a valley two miles from your car, gut it, clean it, butcher it, and extract from it a few dry, nearly tasteless roasts and some faux-baloney.

Here's what may push you over the edge:

HOW TO FIELD CLEAN AND DRESS A BUCK

1. *Cut a circle around the anus* and cut the connecting alimentary canal. Cut as deeply as you can.
2. *Lie the animal on its back* and open the belly from lower body up. Cut along either side of the penis and scrotum.
3. *Cut carefully to loosen the scrotum* and penis, then pull up on the anus—which should by now be detached—and pass it and the alimentary canal through the arch of the pelvis.
4. *Break the membrane over the chest cavity,* reach inside, and scoop out all the organs and entrails.
5. *Put the heart and liver in a plastic bag* to keep from getting blood all over your clothes.
6. *Tip the carcass onto its side* to drain the blood out.
7. *Wipe the body cavity clean* with a cloth or some dry grass.
8. *Prop the body cavity open* with a stick and let it air-dry.

9. ***Next, sew up the body cavity*** so that you can carry it without soiling your clothes. When you're ready to skin the deer, you can remove the stitching.

10. ***Locate hair-tufted glands on the rear legs*** and remove them with a knife. Some hunters say that leaving them on the carcass will taint the meat.

11. ***Hang the buck from a tree branch*** by the neck or antlers. Using a saw or knife, remove all four legs at center joints.

12. ***Take each leg and make a slit on the inside*** all the way to where the belly is open.

13. ***Extend the slit in the belly*** to the brisket and throat, also splitting the breastbone as you go.

14. ***Cut around the neck.*** If you plan to mount the head, cut a little lower to preserve as much of the head and neck as possible.

15. ***Skin the deer by starting high and yanking downward*** on the skin. Use a knife on the tough spots.

THE FINAL VERDICT

While we're all pleased to endorse the idea of walking through the woods well armed, and while most of us wholeheartedly advance the worth of firearms, and, for that matter, all objects of any kind that are capable of making large, obnoxious noises—**the notion of do-it-yourself butchery leaves many men cold.** It's not just the moral problem. After all, most men wear leather belts and eat cheeseburgers—and besides, unless we can reclaim the entire of the earth's surface for critterdom, we have to husband wildlife just as we do other resources. That spells culling to most of us.

No. The problem with hunting—at least for some guys—is what can happen to you once you're out in the field with gun and ammo. Out there, the problem with hunting is that you might actually hit something.

HOW TO HUNT AND GRADE FOOD ON THE CHICKEN SCALE

Another problem with hunting is that for meat eaters, fish don't count. There's beef and there's chicken. After that, there's a whole bunch of stuff that sort of tastes like chicken, more or less, depending on where it registers on the chicken standard. If you're going out hunting for a specific animal—as opposed to hunting for whatever you happen to hit—we have a few specific tactical recommendations, as well as a correlative reading on the official Man's Life Chick-o-Meter. Here, in descending order of chickenlike taste affinity, is the list to take to the big meat shop in the woods: Grouse, turkey, pheasant, quail, duck, frog, woodchuck, deer, rabbit, squirrel, crow, porcupine, raccoon, opossum.

HOW TO AVOID SHOOTING YOURSELF IN THE FOOT

As we said above, however you feel about hunting, hunting hardware is entirely jake. Let's deconstruct the totem of the slain animal and see what kinds of tools it takes to make a man a hunter. We'll start with firearms, go through archery, and come out the other side with knives.

YOU NEVER KNOW

The bad news about guns is that you need absolutely no intention of doing evil to have evil happen. A loaded gun in the hands of a guy you can only describe as a loose cannon is trouble-in-waiting.

The best safety device to attach to a firearm is a big batch of common sense. Here's a no-brainer safety checklist:

- *Figure all firearms are loaded* weapons with broken safety devices.
- *Never point a firearm at anything*—or at anybody—unless you're ready to fire. And take a look at what's behind your target, too.
- *Don't put your finger on the trigger* of a gun until you are ready to fire it.
- *Never hand a firearm to someone else* until you have confirmed that it is unloaded.
- *Never carry a gun with the hammer cocked.*
- *Store guns and ammo* in separate, locked places where no children can get them.
- If you need to keep a loaded firearm with you or nearby, *buy the safest one that you can find,* which should be the one with the most reliable safety.

Clip that list and take it with you when you go to buy a firearm, since buying a gun is not only a consumer issue, it's also a safety issue.

You may also want to take the course in basic firearms safety offered by the National Rifle Association.

A RIFLE MAKES A GOOD FIRST GUN

As a new gun buyer, ***don't trust your first impulse*** about which gun feels best in your hands. The more experience and information you have about firearms, the more demanding your requirements will be, and the one you might have chosen first may end up being your last choice.

- ***Consider buying a .22-caliber rifle as your first firearm.*** Relatively quiet, possessing almost no recoil, a rifle capable of shooting a .22-caliber long-rifle cartridge can do almost anything you need to do with a firearm: You can kill beer cans, eliminate rodents and other pesky critters, dissuade invaders, and vanquish snakes. Even though a .22 is the smallest piece of ammo you can buy, if you fire a .22 long-rifle bullet along a trajectory about thirty degrees above the horizon, it could travel farther than a mile.

- ***Two Trigger Tips***
  1. *Don't jerk the trigger.* You'll lift the rifle and miss your target. Instead of jerking, squeeze the trigger smoothly by concentrating on the movement of your finger, not on the movement of the trigger. This requires patience and practice.
  2. *Take a slow, deep breath,* exhale very slowly, then squeeze the trigger at the bottom of the exhale. You'll be less likely to yank the rifle during firing.

- ***Maintenance***
Everything from the oil and perspiration of your hands to the weather to gunpowder will start breaking down the beautiful appearance of your new rifle almost from the time you get it home. Shoot back: Use wood oils and preservatives to keep your gun looking as new as possible. After each firing, follow this new-rifle cleaning schedule:

> *Clean it every day* for a week.
> *Clean it once a week* for a month.
> *Clean it once a month* forever.

SHOTGUNS

While a rifle shoots a single bullet, a shotgun shoots a whole load of shot. With a rifle, accuracy is paramount because you either hit your target or you don't. With a shotgun, the shot begins to spread out in a V-pattern the minute it is released from the barrel, so hitting a target is a kind of approximate thing, in which "close" counts, sort of like horseshoes and hand grenades. While the range of a shotgun is much, lower than the range achieved with a rifle, the odds of hitting the target are much higher because you're sending out hundreds of projectiles in the direction of the target instead of just one. Because you are sending out bits of shot instead of one bullet, there is no rifling on the inside barrel of a shotgun.

Types: Shotguns come as single-shot, single-barrel automatics, double barrel with a side-by-side configuration, and double barrel with over-and-under configuration. As with rifles, you can get a shotgun that is an automatic or pump. In addition, some shotguns break open for reloading.

- *Shotguns are generally used for bird hunting* and, again because you are shooting many bits of shot instead of a single bullet, you don't sight your target. Instead, you lead it. In other words, you aim the shot along a trajectory ahead of the path of your target. The idea is that the target will fly into the shot—not that the shot will hit the target.

- *The lower the gauge, the heavier the gun.* If you're just starting out, use a 12-gauge, the big, heavy cousin of the relatively svelte 16-gauge. When you've got both of those figured, trade up to a 20-gauge. It's like shooting with a lethal feather.

What to Shoot

When you've killed all the grouse and laid low all the pheasants, you've still got two year-round targets: skeet and trap. Think of it as hunting with a score-card.

- *Trap shooting.* Here's the bit: Five shooters stand in a semicircle and take turns shooting at clay pigeons that are tossed into the air in random directions by a catapult. In a round of trap shooting, each man fires five times from each position, for a total of twenty-five shots. If a guy hits a pigeon, he scores a point.

- *Skeet.* In skeet shooting, the targets come high (from a "high house") and low (from a "low house"). In a typical turn, a pigeon is sent out high, then low, then both, simultaneously. Each shooter gets a total of twenty-four shots, not counting the customary extra shot each guy gets after he takes his first miss.

- *Some places have organized courses* through which shooters progress, taking shots at various target patterns designed to represent different types of real-life prey—pheasant, woodcock, turkey, and so on. You keep score.

  Caution: Women are often better at this than men.

  In any case, the principle of leading and shooting is the same— and so is the object of the game—killing them targets.

How to Shoot a Clay Pigeon

Stop here for a minute to consider the clay pigeon. Always in season, easy to shoot, lousy to eat. Life is full of such compromises, and as compromises go, this isn't a terrible one. But what if they were not only lousy to eat, but hard to shoot? Here's how to prevent a good sport from turning into a bad deal.

- *Some safety notes.* Mind if we repeat this? Use all the gun-and-ammo common sense you've got: Don't point the gun at anybody, don't load it unless you want to shoot it, and don't put your finger on the trigger unless you're ready to pull it.

- *Armed golf.* Shooting clays is like golf with firearms. You want to start relaxed and stay relaxed. Begin by facing the area where you think it's most likely your shot will meet the clay. Then rotate your hips, like a batter, to face the launch area. Hold your shotgun with your right hand comfortably on the butt-grip; when the clay is launched, "mount" the gun by bringing it up to your shoulder and supporting the barrel with your left hand. If you haven't shot for a while, you might want to practice this crucial move a few times before you call for your first clay.

- *Clay Martians.* Once you feel relaxed and ready, yell, "Pull!"— at which time your wife, daughter, neighbor, somebody will fling a small clay target up against the sky. This is where the whole enterprise goes video, since shooting a clay pigeon is like nothing other than shooting a space invader. You watch the path of the target while swinging your gun up and along that same path of flight. At the same time, you mount the shotgun. At the moment the shotgun comes to your shoulder, you should be leading the target by a breath and a half. Now pull the trigger.

- *Be a hoser.* After you squeeze the trigger, don't stop! Think of your shotgun as a garden hose spraying a stream of water along the flight line of the clay—but in this case, of course, you're "spraying" a stream of pellets. As you fire the shot, continue leading the target; this follow-through technique will make all the difference between hit and a miss. Or between a miss and a near-miss. With a little practice, you'll be breaking clay pigeons faster than a senator can say, "Filibuster!"

How to Own Sherwood Forest

You take a dose of green politics, an affection for wishful romanticism, and a decent bow-and-arrow rig, and you've got everything you need to create Robin Hood, an Old Democrat if ever there was one. Add a bunch of federal regs and a health-care motive for stealing from the rich, and you've got a New Democrat. Either way, start with the right bow.

HOW TO SELECT A BOW

When buying a bow, the important thing to consider is the "draw weight" of the bow—the number of pounds of energy that are required to draw a

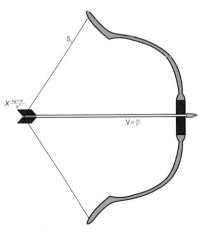

twenty-eight-inch arrow. **Here's how to tell if you have the correct bow weight:** Pull the bow back to a full draw and hold it for ten seconds. If you start shaking before the ten seconds are up, you need to drop down to a lower-weight bow. Most archery rookies start with a thirty- or forty-pounder.

- *If you plan to hunt with the bow,* get one with as much weight as you can handle. The more weight to the bow, the more speed and penetrating power to the arrow shot from it. If what you want to hunt is a large animal—say, a deer—you're going to need at least a fifty-pound bow, at least in most states.

BOW CARE

Because their usefulness depends on their "freshness," or the degree to which they can maintain their shape, bows have to be used and stored with care.

- *Remove the string* when you aren't using the bow.
- *Hang it horizontally* across a couple of pegs.
- *Protect it* with furniture wax if you're going to be using it in wet weather. Dry it after wet-weather use.
- *Warm it up,* especially if you're using the bow in cold air.

HOW TO STRING A BOW

- *One way:* Put one end of the bow on the ground against your foot and push down on the opposite end. Once the bow is flexed enough, slip the string over the end and into the notch.
- *Another way:* Use a bow stringer—a piece of rope, usually nylon, with leather pockets at each end. Slip the pockets over the ends of the bow, then hold the bow parallel to the ground, with the stringer down. Put your foot in the middle of the stringer cord, and lift up on the bow by the handle. See the flex? Slip the string over both ends of the bow and into the nocks. The advantage of a bow stringer is that it puts the same amount of pressure on both sides of the bow.

HOW TO FIND A STRAIGHT ARROW

Get good ammo. Aluminum arrows stink. If you use them when hunting, they make a racket and scare the wildlife. If you hit something hard with them, they're shot. Fiberglas is a better choice—better penetration, longer life, quieter travel.

Your choice of arrows should be as precise as your choice of bows. In arrows, as in some other aspects of life, length is everything. In fact, you can tell how long a guy's arrow is by measuring the distance, fingertip to fingertip, between his outstretched arms.

HOW TO SELECT A KNIFE

Avoid collector's knives, unless, of course, you're a collector. The knife that looks good and the knife that works good are often two different knives. For instance, any blade over five or six inches long is probably too big to be of much use.

Wooden handles handle best. Knives with a solid metal handle look great, but wood is a better choice. A metal handle will get slippery when wet, and when it gets cold, it will be cold for you to hold unless you have gloves on. Wood is a much better material for making a knife useful under difficult conditions.

Here's what to look for in a knife:

- *Durability.* How is the handle attached to the blade? Bolts are best.
- *Cosmetics.* Does the blade have a lot of fancy design work on it? If so, think again, for many manufacturers put more attention into the fancy scrollwork on the blade than they do into the design of the knife.
- *Assembly.* Look at the guard, where the blade meets the handle. Is there a gap between the blade and guard or the guard and the handle? Shouldn't be.
- *Finish.* Look at the finish on the blade. The shinier the blade, the higher the quality.
- *Operation.* If it's a folding knife you are shopping for, listen when you open and close the knife. You should hear a little "click" when

the blade snaps into each position. When the blade is closed, the handle should cover the blade completely, except for the small reveal where the nail slot is located. When the blade is open, you shouldn't be able to wiggle the blade back and forth.

- *Size and fit.* Finally, how does the knife feel in your hand? If you're going to own only one knife, make it one with a three-inch blade.

Carbon vs. stainless steel. Stainless knives cost more than knives made of carbon steel. Although a carbon-steel blade is prone to rusting, it's easier to sharpen and keep clean, provided you follow this four-step waltz with knife maintenance:

1. When it gets wet, dry it.
2. When you put it away, oil it.
3. When you sheath it, avoid leather. Leather pits metal.
4. Once you have it sharp, keep it sharp.

How to Build a Classic Snowman

At twenty below, he's a silent sentinel of sleet and snow. What a guy! Three giant balls and a borrowed top hat, the Pillsbury Doughboy grown up, with frozen testosterone added, a classic man for one season.

Making wintertime's Mr. Right might seem almost instinctive, but there is a spark of divine sensibility required if you want to do the job properly.

- *Go for the gut.* Think of your snowman as a giant, upright, frozen bug—head, thorax, abdomen—but challenged by the apparent absence of several legs. The size of the belly is what will determine the size and shape of the entire snowchap. Here's the ratio of gut-to-torso-to-noggin: 3:1.5:1. That means you need a three-foot ball of snow to start your man off right. The middle ball ought to be about a foot and a half wide, and for the brainpan, you're looking at twelve inches or so.
- *Roll 'em!* Here's where mere mortals mess up the manufacture of their man: Pack a snowball the size of a cantaloupe as tight as God

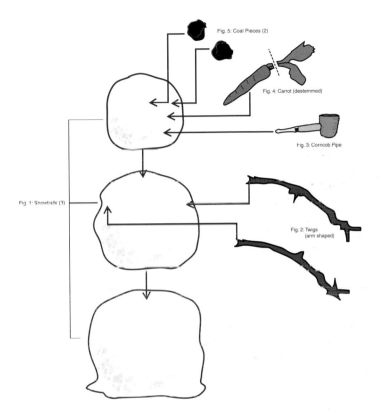

Fig. 5: Coal Pieces (2)

Fig. 4: Carrot (destemmed)

Fig. 3: Corncob Pipe

Fig. 1: Snowballs (3)

Fig. 2: Twigs
(arm shaped)

will permit. Then walk a long, long way away from the post you've assigned your winter lawn jockey. Put your melon-sized ball on the ground and roll it around *slowly*, the way kids roll Play-Doh, the way muggers roll sailors, packing it as you go. When you have a mass measuring about thirty-three to thirty-five inches, roll the big ball to your site. This keeps the snow around the snowman fresh and relatively untramped. Hollow out a spot on the top so that when you put the torso-ball on the belly-ball, it won't roll off. Make the next two parts some distance away from the snowman, and perch them in place atop the first ball.

- ***Accessorize.*** The rubrics for this are familiar, but incorrect: a corncob pipe (see instructions earlier in this chapter), a button nose, and two eyes made out of coal. In reality, the only nose permitted by federal regulations for use by temporary citizens of frozen stature is a carrot. Top hat is suggested—a snowman is not a scarecrow; he may be frozen, but he is formal. Scarf suggested. Twig arms: akimbo, with broom or snow shovel optional. That's it. Stand back and call him Frosty.

8. How to Find the Meaning of Life

Isn't that always the way? You look and look and the darned thing was right in front of you all the time.

Perform an extremity check: To find the meaning of life, simply look at your fingers from time to time and see what they're up to.

- *If you're ten* and holding a bat and some twelve-year-old Visigoth is staring down at you from the mound, the meaning of life can be found at the exact spot where your bat will meet the ball.
- *If you're seventeen* and have somehow found your hand just inches from a small, pert breast, you may believe you have the meaning of life right there in your trousers, a long-term misapprehension that accounts for much distress in men's lives.
- *If you're twenty-eight,* fumbling with a surgical mask and standing next to a somewhat anxious young woman in a delivery room (and you're not an actual obstetrician), you'll soon be able to spot the meaning of life, because he will be the smallest person in the room.
- *If you're forty-five,* you *think* the meaning of life is hidden in a spidery weave of perks and products, ranging from the cellular phone you've got pressed against your ear to the table Vic always saves for you at Club Swank. Your ex-wife and the guy reading your electrocardiogram both think otherwise.
- *If you're sixty,* holding a fishing rod, but still otherwise gainfully employed, you think the meaning of life has something to do with fishing, but not with gainful employment. Unfortunately, you will share this epiphany with friends. At great length.

If, however, you should somehow approach the end of your life without ever having bothered to look for the meaning of it, you can, in a pinch, **use this simple mathematical formula:**

1. *Take the dollar value* of all your IRA, Keogh, 401(k), or other pension plans.
2. *Add the book value* of your savings and other assets.
3. *Divide that subtotal* by the combined ages of all your children.
4. Next, *add up how many times* a woman, not personally known by you, looked you square in the eye and smiled at you in what a reasonable man would consider to be a lascivious manner.
5. *Multiply the total number* of lascivious looks by ten, and divide by the number of divorces among your immediate family. Divide the first number by the second. Now multiply your grand total by the percentage of every thing you think you can take with you.

And there you go.